THE BEST
CAST-IRON
COOKBOOK

THE BEST CAST-IRON COOKBOOK

13-Digit ISBN: 978-1-64643-082-6
10-Digit ISBN: 1-64643-082-4

This book may be ordered by mail from the publisher. Please include $5.99 for postage and handling.
Please support your local bookseller first!

Books published by Cider Mill Press Book Publishers are available at special discounts for bulk purchases in the United States by corporations, institutions, and other organizations. For more information, please contact the publisher.

Cider Mill Press Book Publishers
"Where good books are ready for press"
PO Box 454
12 Spring Street
Kennebunkport, Maine 04046

Visit us online!
cidermillpress.com

Typography: Acumin Pro Condensed, Adobe Garamond Pro, Archer, Black Jack, Brandon Grotesque, Gotham

Photography: Pages 25, 29, 33, 43, 99, 103, 138, 144, 147, 149, 151, 174, and 178 courtesy of Cider Mill Press.
Page 225 © StockFood / Short, Jonathan. Page 229 © StockFood / Richard Jackson Photography.
All other images used under official license from Shutterstock.com.

Front cover image:
Classic Cast-Iron Steak (Preheat oven to 450°F and leave steak out at room temperature for 30 minutes prior to cooking. Heat a large skillet over high heat. Season steak with salt and pepper. Add vegetable oil to hot skillet; when it begins to shimmer, add steak. Lower heat to medium and cook until browned, about 4 minutes on each side. Transfer skillet to the oven. Roast until an instant-read thermometer inserted sideways into the steak registers 120°F for medium-rare, about 6 to 8 minutes. Transfer steak to a cutting board and let it rest for 10 minutes before serving.)

Back cover images:
Country Fried Steaks and Gravy (page 101), Lamb Stew (page 122), Plum Galette (page 231).

Front endpaper image:
Classic Burgers (page 106).

Back endpaper image:
Dutch Apple Baby (page 235).

Printed in China
2 3 4 5 6 7 8 9 0

THE BEST
CAST-IRON
COOKBOOK

125 DELICIOUS RECIPES
FOR YOUR CLASSIC COOKWARE

CIDER MILL PRESS

BOOK
PUBLISHERS

KENNEBUNKPORT, MAINE

TABLE OF CONTENTS

✳ ✳ ✳

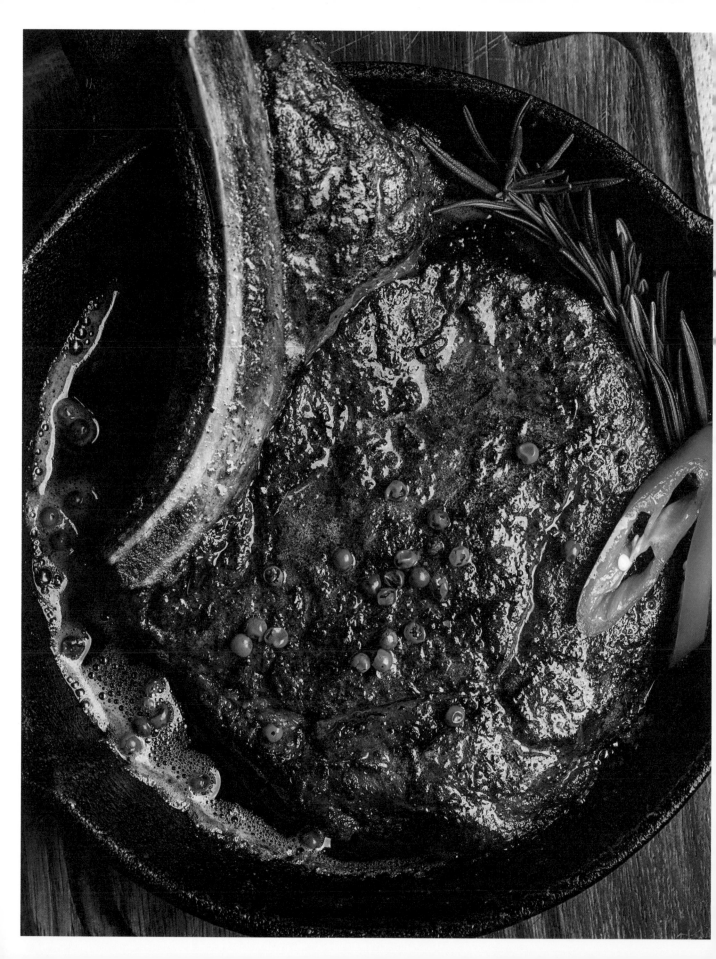

INTRODUCTION

❋ ❋ ❋

Cast-iron cookware is a timeless, versatile, eco-friendly kitchen tool for anyone who likes to cook.

When we're young and learn to cook, cast iron is daunting. We are too weak to lift it, so it is left to the adults in the house. Maybe you grew up watching Sunday pancakes being cooked and expertly flipped in the pan your grandmother used, or maybe you watched someone tend to freshly caught fish as they sizzled in a perfectly seasoned cast-iron skillet that sat over a campfire. Or maybe you also spent chilly winter afternoons in a wooden cabin, après-ski, warming up by a cast-iron stove, waiting patiently for the hot chocolate to be cool enough to take a sip. Such memories drive us to cherish something, to pursue learning more about it, and to find a community that appreciates that which is timeless and aesthetically pleasing.

The other incredible aspect of cast iron is how it's used by people all over the world. In its various forms, cast-iron cookware is a durable and dynamic tool that is an essential part of cuisines loved by people from all walks of life, no matter where they live. In many ways, cast-iron cookware is the melting pot of the world, literally and figuratively.

To anyone who enjoys cooking, a cast-iron pan is a thing of beauty: the form, the weight, the possibilities, the commitment that comes with owning it, and the knowledge that each pan is either already a part of history or has the potential to be. Each pot and pan is a work of art, as proven by every person who has ever decoratively displayed their cookware. In the end, you may choose cast iron because it is practical, can be both inexpensive and expensive, utilitarian, a work of art, a collectible, an heirloom, or an item you intend to pass down to future generations.

CHAPTER 1

BREAKFAST

Sometimes breakfast is as simple as grabbing a piece
of fruit and running out the door. But other times we want, or
really need, to sidle up to the stove and take a few minutes to make
something that is worth lingering over. In other words, a real meal. In
this chapter, you can choose from classics like French Toast with Rum
Bananas (see page 16) to the less traditional, though no less delicious,
like Savory Peanut Butter Oatmeal (see page 24). No matter what you
pick to get your day started you can proceed knowing that, thanks to
your well-seasoned cast iron, cleanup will be easy—meaning
you won't come home to a sink full of dishes.

The Best Breakfast Buns

YIELD: **6 SERVINGS**

ACTIVE TIME: **1 HOUR AND 30 MINUTES**

TOTAL TIME: **2 HOURS**

These take a bit of preparation time, but the result is worth it. Your family or friends will wake up to the smell of these baking, and soon you'll have a kitchen full of people happily waiting for them to come out of the oven.

INGREDIENTS

ALL-PURPOSE FLOUR, FOR DUSTING

1 (26.4 OZ.) PACKAGE OF FROZEN BISCUITS

½ CUP CHOPPED PECANS

1 TEASPOON GROUND CINNAMON

¼ TEASPOON NUTMEG

4 TABLESPOONS UNSALTED BUTTER, SOFTENED

¾ CUP FIRMLY PACKED LIGHT BROWN SUGAR

1 CUP CONFECTIONERS' SUGAR

3 TABLESPOONS HALF-AND-HALF

½ TEASPOON VANILLA EXTRACT

DIRECTIONS

1. Preheat the oven to 375°F.

2. Lightly dust a flat surface with flour. Spread the frozen biscuit dough out in rows of 4 biscuits each. Cover with a kitchen towel and let sit for about 30 minutes, until the dough is thawed but still cool.

3. While dough is thawing, toast the pecans. Spread the pieces on a cookie sheet and bake for about 5 minutes, stirring the pieces with a spatula about halfway through. Be sure not to overcook. Allow to cool. Put the pieces in a bowl and add the cinnamon and nutmeg, stirring to coat the nuts with the spices.

4. Sprinkle flour over the top of the biscuit dough and then press it out to form a large rectangle (approximately 10 by 12 inches). Spread the softened butter over the dough.

5. Sprinkle the brown sugar over the butter, then the seasoned nuts. Roll the dough with the butter, brown sugar, and nuts in it, starting with a long side. Cut into 1-inch slices and place in a lightly greased 10-inch cast-iron skillet.

6. Place in the oven for about 30 to 35 minutes, until the rolls in the center are cooked through. Remove from the oven and allow to cool.

7. Make the glaze by mixing the confectioners' sugar, half-and-half, and vanilla. Drizzle over the warm rolls and serve.

VARIATION: Substitute toasted walnut or almond pieces instead of the pecans for a nuttier, earthier flavor.

Cinnamon Coffee Cake

YIELD: **6 TO 8 SERVINGS**

ACTIVE TIME: **1 HOUR AND 30 MINUTES**

TOTAL TIME: **2 HOURS**

Cinnamon is not only wonderfully fragrant, it is also a natural antioxidant and anti-inflammatory and helps to fight infection.

INGREDIENTS

FOR THE CAKE

1¾ CUPS ALL-PURPOSE FLOUR

⅔ CUP SUGAR

½ TEASPOON BAKING SODA

¼ TEASPOON SALT

¼ TEASPOON GROUND CINNAMON

1 STICK OF UNSALTED BUTTER, AT ROOM TEMPERATURE

2 EGGS

1 TEASPOON VANILLA EXTRACT

¾ CUP BUTTERMILK

FOR THE TOPPING

1 CUP ALL-PURPOSE FLOUR

½ CUP GRANULATED SUGAR

½ CUP DARK BROWN SUGAR

½ TEASPOON CINNAMON

¼ TEASPOON SALT

6 TABLESPOONS UNSALTED BUTTER, AT ROOM TEMPERATURE

DIRECTIONS

1. Preheat the oven to 325°F.

2. To make the cake, whisk together the flour, sugar, baking soda, salt, and cinnamon in a large bowl. Add the butter and mix with a handheld mixer until blended.

3. In a small bowl, whisk together the eggs, vanilla, and buttermilk. Pour into the flour mixture and blend on high speed until the batter is light and fluffy. Pour the batter into a greased, 10-inch cast-iron skillet.

4. To make the topping, whisk together the flour, sugars, cinnamon, and salt in a bowl. Add the butter and combine to form a crumbly dough.

5. Sprinkle the topping over the cake in the skillet. Put the skillet in the oven and bake for 45 minutes, until a knife inserted in the middle comes out clean. Allow to cool for about 10 minutes before serving.

Rosemary & Black Pepper Scones

YIELD: **4 TO 6 SERVINGS**

ACTIVE TIME: **30 MINUTES**

TOTAL TIME: **50 MINUTES**

While these are a bit savory for an early breakfast, they are a hit for brunch, when they can very nicely complement a simple omelette and a Mimosa made with fresh orange juice.

INGREDIENTS

3 CUPS ALL-PURPOSE FLOUR, PLUS MORE FOR DUSTING

2½ TEASPOONS BAKING POWDER

½ TEASPOON BAKING SODA

1 TEASPOON SALT

1½ STICKS OF UNSALTED BUTTER, CHILLED, CUT INTO PIECES

1 TABLESPOON DRIED ROSEMARY

1 TABLESPOON FRESHLY GROUND BLACK PEPPER

1 CUP WHOLE MILK OR HALF-AND-HALF

DIRECTIONS

1. Preheat the oven to 400°F. Position a rack in the middle of the oven.

2. In a large bowl, whisk together the flour, baking powder, baking soda, and salt. Add the butter pieces and mix with an electric mixer until just blended, or mix with a fork so that the dough is somewhat crumbly.

3. Stir in the rosemary, black pepper, and milk or half-and-half, being careful not to overmix.

4. With flour on your hands, transfer the dough to a lightly floured surface. Form the dough into a circle about ½-inch thick. With a long knife, cut the dough into 12 wedges.

5. Butter a 12-inch cast-iron skillet, then place the scone wedges in the skillet in a circle, leaving some space between the pieces. Bake for 20 to 25 minutes, or until golden.

Cheddar & Jalapeño Scones

YIELD: **4 TO 6 SERVINGS**

ACTIVE TIME: **30 MINUTES**

TOTAL TIME: **50 MINUTES**

The spiciness of jalapeño livens up any meal. For an added kick of flavor, split the cooked scones in half and put a spoonful of sour cream and some sliced avocado in the middle.

INGREDIENTS

2 CUPS ALL-PURPOSE FLOUR, PLUS MORE FOR DUSTING

1 TEASPOON BAKING POWDER

½ TEASPOON SALT

1 TEASPOON FRESHLY GROUND BLACK PEPPER

4 TABLESPOONS UNSALTED BUTTER, CHILLED, CUT INTO PIECES

¾ CUP GRATED SHARP CHEDDAR CHEESE

½ CUP SLICED OR CHOPPED JALAPEÑO PEPPER

½ CUP WHOLE MILK

1 EGG, BEATEN WITH A LITTLE MILK

DIRECTIONS

1. Preheat the oven to 400°F. Position a rack in the middle of the oven.

2. In a large bowl, whisk together the flour, baking powder, salt, and black pepper. Add the butter pieces and mix with an electric mixer until just blended, or mix with a fork so that the dough is somewhat crumbly.

3. Stir in the cheese, jalapeño, and milk, being careful not to overmix.

4. With flour on your hands, transfer the dough to a lightly floured surface. Form the dough into a circle about ½-inch thick. With a long knife, cut the dough into 12 wedges.

5. Place the wedges in a circle in a lightly greased 12-inch cast-iron skillet, leaving some space between the pieces.

6. Brush with the beaten egg. Bake for 20 to 25 minutes, or until golden.

VARIATION: Ramp up the heat by substituting Pepper Jack cheese for the cheddar, or substitute a serrano pepper for the jalapeño.

French Toast with Rum Bananas

YIELD: **4 TO 6 SERVINGS**

ACTIVE TIME: **10 MINUTES**

TOTAL TIME: **10 MINUTES**

The ultimate pairing of decadent breakfast and sweet, boozy dessert, this combination of two classics is sure to win over everyone.

INGREDIENTS

FOR THE FRENCH TOAST

3 TABLESPOONS UNSALTED BUTTER

8 EGGS

2 TABLESPOONS SUGAR

½ CUP HEAVY CREAM

1 TABLESPOON CINNAMON

1 TABLESPOON VANILLA EXTRACT

PINCH OF SALT

1 LOAF OF BRIOCHE, CUT INTO 10 TO 12 SLICES

FOR THE BANANAS FOSTER

1 STICK OF UNSALTED BUTTER

½ CUP LIGHT BROWN SUGAR, PACKED

3 BANANAS, SLICED

¼ CUP DARK RUM

½ CUP HEAVY CREAM

POWDERED SUGAR, FOR TOPPING

DIRECTIONS

1. Preheat the oven to 200°F and place an ovenproof dish in it. Heat a 12-inch cast-iron skillet over medium-high heat and melt 1 tablespoon of butter per batch of French toast.

2. In a bowl, add the eggs, sugar, heavy cream, cinnamon, vanilla, and salt and stir to combine. Dunk the slices of bread in the batter to cover both sides. Cook the bread in batches for 1 minute per side, or until a light brown crust forms. Remove from the pan and keep warm in the oven.

3. Place the skillet over medium-high heat and start to prepare the bananas Foster. Add the stick of butter and the brown sugar.

4. Once the butter and sugar are melted, add the bananas to the pan and cook for 3 minutes. Shake the pan and use a spoon to cover the bananas with the sauce.

5. Pull the pan away from the heat and add the rum. Using a long match or lighter, carefully light the rum on fire. Place the pan back over the heat and shake the pan until the flames are gone.

6. Add the cream. Stir to blend and pour over the French toast. Sprinkle with powdered sugar and serve.

TIP: When adding alcohol to hot pans, make sure you pull them away from heat before adding the alcohol. This will help you avoid potential fires and injuries.

Apple Pancake

YIELD: **4 TO 6 SERVINGS**

ACTIVE TIME: **30 MINUTES**

TOTAL TIME: **1 HOUR**

Make this the morning after you go apple picking. It's a great way to use up some of the apples and get your day off to a great start.

INGREDIENTS

4 EGGS

1 CUP WHOLE MILK

3 TABLESPOONS SUGAR

½ TEASPOON VANILLA EXTRACT

½ TEASPOON SALT

¾ CUP ALL-PURPOSE FLOUR

4 TABLESPOONS UNSALTED BUTTER

2 APPLES, PEELED, CORED, AND SLICED THIN

¼ TEASPOON CINNAMON

DASH OF GROUND NUTMEG

DASH OF GROUND GINGER

¼ CUP LIGHT BROWN SUGAR

CONFECTIONERS' SUGAR, FOR SPRINKLING (OPTIONAL)

DIRECTIONS

1. Preheat the oven to 425°F.

2. In a large bowl, whisk together the eggs, milk, sugar, vanilla, and salt. Add the flour and whisk to combine. Set the batter aside.

3. Place a 12-inch cast-iron skillet over medium-high heat and add the butter, tilting the pan to thoroughly coat the bottom. Add the apple slices and top with the cinnamon, nutmeg, and ginger. Cook, while stirring, until apples begin to soften, about 5 minutes. Add the brown sugar and continue to stir while cooking for an additional few minutes, until the apples are very soft. Pat the cooked apples along the bottom of the skillet to distribute evenly.

4. Pour the batter over the apples, coating them evenly. Transfer the skillet to the oven and bake for about 20 minutes, until the pancake is browned and puffy. Sprinkle with confectioners' sugar when fresh out of the oven, if desired. Serve immediately.

VARIATION: To make a gluten-free version of this recipe, just substitute the ¾ cup of flour with ¾ cup Gluten Free All-Purpose Baking Flour from Bob's Red Mill and add 1 teaspoon of xanthan gum. Mix together before whisking into your wet ingredients.

Classic Cast-Iron Pancake

YIELD: **4 SERVINGS**

ACTIVE TIME: **30 MINUTES**

TOTAL TIME: **30 MINUTES**

This recipe was published in the **New York Times** *years ago and has quite the following. It's more of a popover than a traditional pancake, but it's a delicious tribute to writer and editor David Eyre.*

INGREDIENTS

½ CUP ALL-PURPOSE FLOUR

½ CUP WHOLE MILK

2 EGGS, LIGHTLY BEATEN

PINCH OF NUTMEG

4 TABLESPOONS UNSALTED BUTTER

2 TABLESPOONS CONFECTIONERS' SUGAR

JUICE OF ½ LEMON

JAM, FOR SERVING

DIRECTIONS

1. Preheat the oven to 425°F.

2. In a bowl, combine the flour, milk, eggs, and nutmeg. Beat lightly; leave the batter a little lumpy.

3. Melt the butter in a 12-inch cast-iron skillet and, when very hot, pour in the batter.

4. Transfer the skillet to the oven and bake for 15 to 20 minutes, until golden brown.

5. Sprinkle with the sugar, return briefly to the oven, then remove. Sprinkle with lemon juice and serve with your favorite jam.

Porridge with Dried Fruit

YIELD: **4 SERVINGS**

ACTIVE TIME: **5 MINUTES**

TOTAL TIME: **30 MINUTES**

This dish is all about mastering the method. Try this recipe as suggested, and then take all of the liberties you can think of, swapping in any grain, dried fruit, and milk that you want.

INGREDIENTS

1 CUP BUCKWHEAT GROATS

1 CUP STEEL-CUT OATS

2 TABLESPOONS FLAX SEEDS

2 TEASPOONS CINNAMON

1 CUP CHOPPED DRIED FRUIT (APPLES, APRICOTS, PINEAPPLE, DATES, ETC.)

2 CUPS WATER

2 CUPS ALMOND MILK

1 GRANNY SMITH APPLE, FOR GARNISH

¼ CUP CHOPPED ALMONDS, FOR GARNISH

DIRECTIONS

1. Place all of the ingredients, other than the Granny Smith apple and the almonds, in a cast-iron Dutch oven.

2. Bring to a gentle simmer and cover. Cook, while stirring occasionally to prevent the porridge from sticking to the bottom, for 20 minutes.

3. Remove the porridge from heat and ladle into warm bowls. Peel the apple and grate it over each bowl. Top with the chopped almonds and serve.

Cheesy Grits

YIELD: **8 TO 10 SERVINGS**

ACTIVE TIME: **15 MINUTES**

TOTAL TIME: **45 MINUTES**

Thelma Goodrich hailed from Dallas, Texas, and she always made this simple dish for special occasions. She passed it on to her granddaughter, Briana Chalais, who says it remains the most popular dish at family gatherings. Once you try it, you'll see why. The beauty of cast iron is on full display here, as it lends the bottom a gorgeous burnish.

INGREDIENTS

4 CUPS WATER

1 CUP QUICK-COOKING GRITS

2 LARGE EGGS

4 TABLESPOONS UNSALTED BUTTER, AT ROOM TEMPERATURE

¾ CUP WHOLE MILK

SALT AND PEPPER, TO TASTE

1 LB. CHEDDAR CHEESE, GRATED

DIRECTIONS

1. Preheat the oven to 425°F.

2. Place the water in a saucepan and bring to a boil. While stirring constantly, slowly add the grits. Cover, reduce the heat to low, and cook, while stirring occasionally, until the grits are quite thick, about 5 minutes. Remove from heat.

3. Place the eggs, butter, and milk in a bowl, season with salt and pepper, and stir to combine. Stir the cooked grits into the egg mixture, add three-quarters of the cheese, and stir to incorporate.

4. Pour the mixture into a greased cast-iron baking dish or skillet, place in the oven, and bake for 30 minutes. Remove, sprinkle the remaining cheese on top, and return the grits to the oven. Bake until the cheese is melted and the grits are firm, about 15 minutes. Remove from the oven and let cool slightly before cutting into squares and serving.

Savory Peanut Butter Oatmeal

YIELD: **4 TO 6 SERVINGS**

ACTIVE TIME: **5 MINUTES**

TOTAL TIME: **20 MINUTES**

Peanut butter, bacon, and eggs in oats? It may sound crazy at first, but the saltiness of the crispy bacon, the texture added by the peanut butter, and the creaminess of the egg yolk work really well together, creating a brand-new take on oatmeal.

INGREDIENTS

6 SLICES OF THICK-CUT BACON

6 EGGS

2 CUPS OATS

6 CUPS WATER

1 TABLESPOON KOSHER SALT

¼ CUP PEANUT BUTTER OF YOUR CHOICE

DIRECTIONS

1. Cook the bacon in a 10-inch cast-iron skillet over medium heat. Remove the bacon from the pan and use the bacon fat to fry the eggs.

2. When the eggs have been fried, remove them from the pan and set aside. Wipe remaining grease from the pan with a paper towel. Add oats, water, and salt and cook over medium heat for 7 to 10 minutes, or until oats are the desired consistency.

3. While the oats are cooking, chop the bacon. Add the bacon and peanut butter to the oatmeal and stir to combine.

4. Top each portion with a fried egg and serve.

Huevos Rancheros

YIELD: **4 SERVINGS**

ACTIVE TIME: **25 MINUTES**

TOTAL TIME: **40 MINUTES**

You can make this a one-dish meal by cutting the tortillas into ½-inch pieces and frying them. Once they've crisped up, spoon the beans and butter over them, pressing them into the bottom of the skillet to brown. Break the eggs over the beans and cover so that the eggs start to set. Cook for about 2 minutes. Take off the lid, cover with cheese, and serve.

INGREDIENTS

2 TABLESPOONS VEGETABLE OIL

4 CORN TORTILLAS (SEE PAGE 62)

½ LB. BLACK OR REFRIED BEANS

1 TABLESPOON UNSALTED BUTTER

4 EGGS

½ CUP GRATED SHARP CHEDDAR CHEESE

½ CUP COTIJA OR GRATED MONTEREY JACK CHEESE

½ CUP FRESH SALSA, FOR SERVING

JALAPEÑO PEPPERS, SLICED, FOR SERVING

FRESH CILANTRO, CHOPPED, FOR SERVING

DIRECTIONS

1. Heat the oil in a 10-inch cast-iron skillet over medium-high heat. Fry the tortillas, one at a time, until firm but not crisp. Transfer cooked tortillas to a plate lined with a paper towel, and separate with paper towels while cooking.

2. Put the beans and butter in a bowl and heat in the microwave for about 1 minute, stirring halfway through.

3. Fry the eggs in the skillet over easy and, once nearly cooked, sprinkle with cheese so that the cheese melts.

4. Place a crispy tortilla on a plate, top with the beans and eggs, and serve hot with the salsa, jalapeños, and cilantro.

Steak & Onion Frittata

YIELD: **6 SERVINGS**

ACTIVE TIME: **10 MINUTES**

TOTAL TIME: **25 MINUTES**

Frittatas are traditionally enjoyed at breakfast, but this one is hearty enough to work any time of day. Serve this with a salad of arugula and red onions for a quick on-the-go lunch if you find yourself pressed for time.

INGREDIENTS

2 TABLESPOONS OLIVE OIL

1 LB. PEARL ONIONS

SALT AND PEPPER, TO TASTE

12 LARGE EGGS

½ CUP HEAVY CREAM OR HALF-AND-HALF

1 (7 TO 8 OZ.) STRIP STEAK, MINCED

4 TABLESPOONS UNSALTED BUTTER

2 TABLESPOONS CHOPPED FRESH PARSLEY

2 CUPS SHREDDED PARMESAN OR ASIAGO CHEESE

DIRECTIONS

1. Preheat oven to 400°F. Place a 10-inch cast-iron skillet over medium-high heat and add the olive oil. Once the pan is hot, add the pearl onions, salt, and pepper and cook until onions start to caramelize, about 5 to 7 minutes.

2. While the onions are cooking, place the eggs, cream or half-and-half, salt, and pepper in a bowl and scramble until combined.

3. Add the steak to the pan with the onions and cook until steak is cooked through, about 2 to 3 minutes. Add the butter and parsley and stir until the butter is melted. Sprinkle the cheese evenly over the onions and steak, then pour the egg mixture into the pan. The eggs should just cover everything else in the pan. Place the skillet in the oven and cook for 8 minutes.

4. Turn the broiler on and cook for another 3 minutes, until the top of the frittata is brown. Remove from the oven and serve.

Savory Strata

YIELD: **4 TO 6 SERVINGS**

ACTIVE TIME: **20 MINUTES**

TOTAL TIME: **1 HOUR**

A nourishing nibble that makes for a filling breakfast, brunch, or lunch. As long as the base includes eggs, milk, bread, and cheese, the remainder can be tailored to personal taste. It's the ideal way to use up leftovers or, in this case, showcase the flawless combination of ham and Swiss cheese.

INGREDIENTS

7 EGGS, BEATEN

2 CUPS WHOLE MILK

½ CUP GRATED SWISS CHEESE

LARGE PINCH OF GROUND NUTMEG

3 CUPS BREAD CUBES

½ CUP DICED HAM OR COOKED BACON

1 YELLOW ONION, MINCED

¼ CUP CHOPPED SPINACH

SALT AND PEPPER, TO TASTE

2 TEASPOONS OLIVE OIL

DIRECTIONS

1. Place the eggs and milk in a large mixing bowl and stir to combine. Add the cheese and nutmeg and stir to incorporate. Add the bread cubes, transfer the mixture to the refrigerator, and chill for 30 minutes.

2. Preheat the oven to 400°F.

3. Add the ham or bacon, onion, and spinach to the egg-and-bread mixture and stir until evenly distributed. Season with salt and pepper.

4. Coat a 10-inch cast-iron skillet with the olive oil. Pour in the strata, place the skillet in the oven, and bake for 25 minutes.

5. Remove from the oven and let cool for 10 minutes before cutting into wedges and serving.

Smoky Sweet Potato Hash

YIELD: **4 TO 6 SERVINGS**

ACTIVE TIME: **20 MINUTES**

TOTAL TIME: **13 TO 17 HOURS**

The sweet, savory, and spicy combination of the lamb and sweet potato puts traditional breakfast hash to shame, and there's nothing wrong with drizzling a little maple syrup over the top to satisfy your midmorning sweet tooth.

INGREDIENTS

FOR THE MARINADE

4 GARLIC CLOVES, PUREED

LEAVES FROM 3 SPRIGS OF OREGANO, MINCED

¼ CUP DIJON MUSTARD

¼ CUP CABERNET SAUVIGNON

1 TABLESPOON KOSHER SALT

1 TABLESPOON CRACKED BLACK PEPPER

FOR THE LAMB

1½ LBS. LEG OF LAMB, BUTTERFLIED

2 TABLESPOONS BEEF TALLOW OR CLARIFIED BUTTER

2 CUPS WATER

FOR THE SWEET POTATO HASH

2 SWEET POTATOES, PEELED AND MINCED

2 TABLESPOONS BEEF TALLOW OR CLARIFIED BUTTER

Continued...

DIRECTIONS

1. To prepare the marinade, combine all of the ingredients in a small bowl and transfer to a 1-gallon resealable bag. Place the lamb in the bag, squeeze all of the air out of the bag, and place in the refrigerator for 12 to 16 hours.

2. To prepare the lamb, preheat the oven to 350°F. Place a cast-iron Dutch oven over medium-high heat and add the beef tallow or clarified butter. Remove the lamb from the bag, place in the pot, and sear for 5 minutes on each side.

3. Add the water to the pot, place it in the oven, and cook for 20 minutes, or until the center of the lamb reaches 140°F on an instant-read thermometer. Remove the pot from the oven, set the lamb aside, and drain the liquid from the pot. Let the lamb sit for 15 minutes, then mince.

4. To prepare the sweet potato hash, fill the pot with water and bring to a boil. Add the sweet potatoes and cook until they are just tender, about 5 minutes. Be careful not to overcook them, as you don't want to end up with mashed potatoes. Drain potatoes and set aside.

5. Add the beef tallow or clarified butter, the poblano peppers, onions, garlic, and cumin to the pot and cook over medium heat until all of the vegetables are soft, about 10 minutes.

6. Return the potatoes and the lamb to the pot. Add the salt and cook for another 15 minutes. Add the oregano, season with salt and black pepper, and serve.

2 POBLANO PEPPERS, DICED (FOR MORE HEAT, SUBSTITUTE 1 LARGE JALAPEÑO PEPPER FOR ONE OF THE POBLANOS)

2 YELLOW ONIONS, MINCED

2-3 GARLIC CLOVES, MINCED

1 TABLESPOON CUMIN

1 TABLESPOON CHOPPED FRESH OREGANO

1 TABLESPOON KOSHER SALT, PLUS MORE TO TASTE

FRESHLY GROUND BLACK PEPPER, TO TASTE

Corned Beef Hash

YIELD: **4 SERVINGS**

ACTIVE TIME: **15 MINUTES**

TOTAL TIME: **35 MINUTES**

Start your day out right with this hearty breakfast hash. The recipe originated in the 1950s and the name comes from the French word hacher, *which means "to chop." If roast beef is easier to come by than corned beef, feel free to use that.*

INGREDIENTS

5 TABLESPOONS VEGETABLE OIL

2 YUKON GOLD POTATOES, DICED INTO ¼-INCH CUBES

1 YELLOW ONION, SLICED INTO THIN HALF-MOONS

1 RED OR GREEN BELL PEPPER, SEEDED AND SLICED THIN

1½ LBS. COOKED CORNED BEEF, DICED

1 CUP TOMATO SAUCE

2 TABLESPOONS TOMATO PASTE

1 TEASPOON HOT SAUCE

4 LARGE EGGS

CHIVES, CHOPPED, FOR GARNISH

DIRECTIONS

1. Place 3 tablespoons of the vegetable oil in a 12-inch cast-iron skillet and warm over medium-high heat. When the oil is shimmering, add the potatoes and cook, while stirring occasionally, until they are golden brown, about 10 minutes.

2. Reduce the heat to medium and add the onion and bell pepper. Cook, while stirring occasionally, for 2 minutes. Add the corned beef and cook until browned, about 8 minutes. Pour in the tomato sauce, tomato paste, and hot sauce, stir to coat, and allow the hash to simmer, while stirring occasionally, for 15 minutes.

3. While the hash is simmering, place the remaining vegetable oil in another cast-iron skillet and warm over medium heat. When the oil is shimmering, crack the eggs into the skillet and cook until the whites are cooked through. To cut down on dishes, you can also make four indentations in the hash, crack the eggs into them, and cook until the whites are set.

4. To serve, spoon the hash onto plates and top each portion with a fried egg. Sprinkle the chives on top and serve immediately.

CHAPTER 2

BREADS & FLATBREADS

From mouthwatering Biscuits (see page 41) to
simply perfect Whole Wheat Bread (see page 42), cast iron
is your bread-making pal, able to elicit those beautiful
blisters, a crispy crust, and a golden edge.

Whole Wheat Cranberry & Pecan Bread

YIELD: **1 SMALL LOAF**

ACTIVE TIME: **25 MINUTES**

TOTAL TIME: **3 HOURS**

This is a delicious, dense bread that is especially good toasted and served with fresh butter or cream cheese. It also makes a great complement to soft cheeses when cut into small pieces and served in place of crackers.

INGREDIENTS

¼ TEASPOON INSTANT YEAST

¼ TEASPOON SUGAR

1½ CUPS WATER (110° TO 115°F)

1 TEASPOON KOSHER SALT

2 CUPS WHOLE WHEAT FLOUR

1 CUP ALL-PURPOSE FLOUR, PLUS MORE FOR DUSTING

1 CUP DRIED CRANBERRIES

1 CUP CHOPPED PECANS

DIRECTIONS

1. Put the yeast and sugar in a measuring cup and drizzle in about ½ cup warm water. Hot water will kill the yeast, so it's important that the water be warm without being hot. Cover the measuring cup with plastic wrap and set it aside for about 15 minutes. If the yeast doesn't foam, it is not alive and you'll need to start over.

2. When the yeast is proofed, pour it into a large bowl and add the remaining cup of warm water. Stir gently to combine. Combine the whole wheat flour and the all-purpose flour in a bowl. Add the salt to the flours, and then add the flour mixture to the yeast mixture. Stir with a wooden spoon until combined. The dough will be wet and sticky.

3. Put a dusting of all-purpose flour on a flat surface and lift out the dough. With flour on your hands and more at the ready, begin kneading the dough so that it loses its stickiness. As you're kneading, add in the cranberries and pecans so that they're distributed evenly in the dough. Don't overdo it, and don't use too much flour, just enough that the dough becomes more cohesive, about 5 minutes.

4. Place the dough in a large bowl, cover the bowl with plastic wrap, and allow to rise untouched until it has roughly doubled in size, at least 1 hour and up to several hours. Gently punch it down, score the top with a sharp knife, re-cover with the plastic, and allow to rise again for another 30 minutes or so.

Continued...

5. While the dough is on its final rise, preheat the oven to 450°F. Put a piece of parchment paper on the bottom of a cast-iron Dutch oven and put it in the oven with the lid on so it gets hot. When the oven is ready and the dough has risen, carefully remove the lid and gently scoop the dough from the bowl into the pot, scored side up. Cover and bake for 15 minutes. Remove the lid and continue to bake for another 15 to 20 minutes, until the top is golden and it sounds hollow when tapped.

6. Remove the pot from the oven and use kitchen towels to carefully remove the bread. Allow to cool before slicing.

Biscuits

YIELD: **4 TO 6 SERVINGS**

ACTIVE TIME: **20 MINUTES**

TOTAL TIME: **40 MINUTES**

For fluffy buttermilk biscuits, you need to work with a very hot skillet. The golden crust on the bottom is as much of a delight as the airy, warm dough.

INGREDIENTS

2 CUPS ALL-PURPOSE FLOUR, PLUS MORE FOR DUSTING

1 TEASPOON SUGAR

1 TEASPOON SALT

1 TABLESPOON BAKING POWDER

1 STICK OF UNSALTED BUTTER, CUT INTO PIECES

½ CUP BUTTERMILK, PLUS 2 TABLESPOONS

DIRECTIONS

1. Preheat oven to 450°F.

2. In a large bowl, combine the flour, sugar, salt, and baking powder.

3. Using a fork or pastry knife, blend in 6 tablespoons of the butter to form a crumbly dough. Form a well in the middle and add ½ cup of the buttermilk. Stir to combine and form a stiff dough. Using your fingers works best! If it seems too dry, add 1 tablespoon more of the buttermilk, going to 2 tablespoons if necessary.

4. Put the remaining butter in a 12-inch cast-iron skillet and put the skillet in the oven.

5. Put the dough on a lightly floured surface and press out to a thickness of about 1 inch. Cut out biscuits using an inverted water glass. Place the biscuits in the skillet and bake for about 10 minutes, until golden on the bottom.

Whole Wheat Bread

YIELD: **1 LOAF**

ACTIVE TIME: **30 MINUTES**

TOTAL TIME: **21 HOURS**

Bread making is a delicate art, as the wrong measurements can lead to a flat loaf and a disappointed baker. That being said, this whole wheat masterpiece will leave no one disappointed, especially when it's served while still warm with plenty of farm-fresh butter.

INGREDIENTS

3¼ CUPS ALL-PURPOSE FLOUR, PLUS MORE FOR DUSTING

1¼ CUPS WHOLE WHEAT FLOUR

1½ CUPS WATER (90°F)

JUST UNDER ¼ TEASPOON ACTIVE DRY YEAST

2¼ TEASPOONS SALT

DIRECTIONS

1. Place the flours and water in a large mixing bowl and use your hands to combine the mixture into a dough. Cover the bowl with a kitchen towel and let the mixture set for 45 minutes to 1 hour.

2. Sprinkle the yeast and salt over the dough and fold until they have been incorporated. Cover the bowl with the kitchen towel and let stand for 30 minutes. Remove the towel, fold a corner of the dough into the center, and cover. Repeat every 30 minutes until all of the corners have been folded in.

3. After the last fold, cover the dough with the kitchen towel and let it sit for 12 to 14 hours.

4. Dust a work surface lightly with flour and place the dough on it. Fold each corner of the dough into the center, flip the dough over, and roll it into a smooth ball. Dust your hands with flour as needed. Be careful not to roll or press the dough too hard, as this will prevent the dough from expanding properly. Dust a bowl with flour and place the dough, seam side down, in the bowl. Let stand until it has roughly doubled in size, about 1 hour and 15 minutes.

5. Cut a round piece of parchment paper that is 1" larger than the circumference of your cast-iron Dutch oven. When the dough has approximately 1 hour left in its rise (this is also known as "proofing"), preheat the oven to 475°F and place the covered Dutch oven in the oven as it warms.

Continued...

6. When the dough has roughly doubled in size, invert it onto a lightly floured work surface. Use a very sharp knife to score one side of the loaf. Using oven mitts, remove the Dutch oven from the oven. Use a bench scraper to transfer the dough onto the piece of parchment, scored side up. Hold the sides of the parchment and carefully lower the dough into the Dutch oven. Cover the Dutch oven and place it in the oven for 20 minutes.

7. Remove the lid and bake the loaf for an additional 20 minutes. Remove from the oven and let cool on a wire rack for at least 2 hours before slicing.

Farmer's White Bread

YIELD: **1 LOAF**

ACTIVE TIME: **30 MINUTES**

TOTAL TIME: **21 HOURS**

Don't be thrown by the "white" in the name. Letting the dough rest overnight allows an incredible amount of flavor to develop, resulting in a loaf that is anything but bland.

INGREDIENTS

4½ CUPS ALL-PURPOSE FLOUR, PLUS MORE FOR DUSTING

1½ CUPS WATER (90°F)

JUST UNDER ¼ TEASPOON ACTIVE DRY YEAST

2¼ TEASPOONS SALT

DIRECTIONS

1. Place the flour and water in a large mixing bowl and use your hands to combine the mixture into a dough. Cover the bowl with a kitchen towel and let the mixture set for 45 minutes to 1 hour.

2. Sprinkle the yeast and salt over the dough and fold until they have been incorporated. Cover the bowl with the kitchen towel and let stand for 30 minutes. Remove the towel, fold a corner of the dough into the center, and cover. Repeat every 30 minutes until all of the corners have been folded in.

3. After the last fold, cover the dough with the kitchen towel and let it sit for 12 to 14 hours.

4. Dust a work surface lightly with flour and place the dough on it. Fold each corner of the dough to the center, flip the dough over, and roll it into a smooth ball. Dust your hands with flour as needed. Be careful not to roll or press the dough too hard, as this will prevent the dough from expanding properly. Dust a bowl with flour and place the dough, seam side down, in the bowl. Let stand until it has roughly doubled in size, about 1 hour and 15 minutes.

5. Cut a round piece of parchment paper that is 1" larger than the circumference of your cast-iron Dutch oven. When the dough has approximately 1 hour left in its rise (this is also known as "proofing"), preheat the oven to 475°F and place the covered Dutch oven in the oven as it warms.

Continued...

6. When the dough has roughly doubled in size, invert it onto a lightly floured work surface. Use a very sharp knife to score one side of the loaf. Using oven mitts, remove the Dutch oven from the oven. Use a bench scraper to transfer the dough onto the piece of parchment, scored side up. Hold the sides of the parchment and carefully lower the dough into the Dutch oven.

Cover the Dutch oven and place it in the oven for 20 minutes.

7. Remove the lid and bake the loaf for an additional 20 minutes. Remove from the oven and let cool on a wire rack for at least 2 hours before slicing.

No-Knead Bread

YIELD: **1 SMALL LOAF**

ACTIVE TIME: **20 MINUTES**

TOTAL TIME: **24 HOURS**

Use a 7-quart cast-iron Dutch oven for this recipe. This delicious bread is a great way to upgrade a pimento cheese sandwich—there is really nothing easier. Just remember that it takes up to two days to make, so plan ahead!

INGREDIENTS

½ TABLESPOON ACTIVE DRY YEAST

¼ TEASPOON SUGAR

1½ CUPS WATER (110° TO 115°F)

1½ TEASPOONS KOSHER SALT

3 CUPS ALL-PURPOSE FLOUR, PLUS MORE FOR DUSTING

DIRECTIONS

1. In a large bowl, add the yeast and sugar and top with the warm water. Stir to dissolve the yeast. Cover the measuring cup with plastic wrap and set it aside for about 15 minutes. If the yeast doesn't foam, it is not alive and you'll need to start over.

2. When the yeast is proofed, add the salt and flour. Stir until just blended with the yeast, sugar, and water. The dough will be sticky.

3. Cover the bowl with plastic wrap and set aside for at least 15 hours and up to 18 hours, preferably in a place that's 65° to 70°F.

4. The dough will be bubbly when you go to work with it. Lightly dust a work surface with flour and scoop the dough out onto it. Dust your fingers with flour so they don't stick to the dough. Fold it gently once or twice.

5. Transfer the dough to a clean, room-temperature bowl and cover with a kitchen towel. Let stand until doubled in size, another 1 to 2 hours.

6. While the dough is on its final rise, preheat the oven to 450°F, placing a cast-iron Dutch oven inside with the lid on so it gets hot. When the oven is ready and the dough has risen, carefully remove the lid and gently scoop the dough from the bowl into the Dutch oven. Cover and bake for 20 minutes. Remove the lid and continue to bake for another 25 minutes, until the top is golden and it sounds hollow when tapped.

7. Remove the Dutch oven from the oven and use kitchen towels to carefully transfer bread to a rack or cutting board. Allow to cool at least 20 minutes before serving.

Irish Soda Bread

YIELD: 1 LOAF

ACTIVE TIME: **30 MINUTES**

TOTAL TIME: **1 HOUR AND 30 MINUTES**

It wouldn't be St. Patrick's Day without soda bread. According to the Culinary Institute of America: "With a history spanning more than two centuries, soda bread is a traditional Irish specialty. The first loaf, consisting of little more than flour, baking soda, salt, and sour milk, made its debut in the mid-1800s when baking soda found its way into Irish kitchens." Make this on a weekend morning when you have some extra time, then have slices of it later in the day with a cup of coffee or tea.

INGREDIENTS

4 CUPS ALL-PURPOSE FLOUR

½ CUP SUGAR

⅛ TEASPOON SALT

3¼ TEASPOONS BAKING POWDER

½ TEASPOON BAKING SODA

2 TABLESPOONS CARAWAY SEEDS

2 LARGE EGGS, LIGHTLY BEATEN

1½ CUPS BUTTERMILK

½ LB. RAISINS

UNSALTED BUTTER FOR THE SKILLET, PLUS MORE FOR SERVING

ORANGE MARMALADE, FOR SERVING

DIRECTIONS

1. Preheat the oven to 450°F.

2. Combine the flour, sugar, salt, baking powder, baking soda, and caraway seeds in a large mixing bowl. Add the beaten eggs and stir to combine. Gradually add the buttermilk until the dough is sticky and messy. Stir in the raisins.

3. Generously butter a 10-inch cast-iron skillet. Scoop and spread the dough in it.

4. Place the skillet in the oven and bake for about 1 hour, until the top is crusty and brown and the bread sounds hollow when tapped. Insert a toothpick in the center to be sure the dough is cooked through; the toothpick should come out clean.

5. Remove from the oven, let cool slightly, and serve with fresh butter and orange marmalade.

Olive Bread

YIELD: **1 SMALL LOAF**

ACTIVE TIME: **25 MINUTES**

TOTAL TIME: **3 HOURS**

The earthy-salty flavor of dark olives like Kalamatas is delicious in bread. If you don't want to take the time to slice a lot of olives, use a top-shelf tapenade spread, which is easy to distribute in the dough.

INGREDIENTS

¼ TEASPOON INSTANT YEAST

¼ TEASPOON SUGAR

1½ CUPS WATER (110° TO 115°F)

1 TEASPOON KOSHER SALT

3 CUPS ALL-PURPOSE FLOUR, PLUS MORE FOR DUSTING

½ CUP SLICED KALAMATA OLIVES OR TAPENADE

1 TABLESPOON OLIVE OIL

DIRECTIONS

1. Put the yeast and sugar in a measuring cup and drizzle in about ½ cup warm water. Hot water will kill the yeast, so it's important that the water be warm without being hot. Cover the measuring cup with plastic wrap and set it aside for about 15 minutes. If the yeast doesn't foam, it is not alive and you'll need to start over.

2. When the yeast is proofed, pour it into a large bowl and add the remaining cup of warm water. Stir gently to combine. Add the salt to the flour and add the dry mixture to the yeast mixture. Stir with a wooden spoon until combined. The dough will be wet and sticky.

3. Put a dusting of flour on a flat surface and lift out the dough. With flour on your hands and more at the ready, begin kneading the dough so that it loses its stickiness. Don't overdo it, and don't use too much flour, just enough that it becomes more cohesive, about 5 minutes. Incorporate the tapenade or olive pieces while you're kneading.

4. Place the dough in a large bowl, cover the bowl with plastic wrap, and allow to rise untouched for at least 1 hour and up to several hours, until doubled in size. Gently punch it down, re-cover with the plastic, and allow to rise again for another 30 minutes or so. Brush with the olive oil.

Continued...

5. While the dough is on its final rise, preheat the oven to 450°F. Put a piece of parchment paper on the bottom of a cast-iron Dutch oven and put it in the oven with the lid on so it gets hot. When the oven is ready and the dough has risen, carefully remove the lid and gently scoop the dough from the bowl into the pot. Cover and bake for 15 minutes. Remove the lid and continue to bake for another 15 to 20 minutes, until the top is golden and it sounds hollow when tapped.

6. Remove the pot from the oven and use kitchen towels to carefully remove the bread from the Dutch oven. Let the loaf cool completely before slicing.

Onion Focaccia

Caramelized onions, when sautéed in butter and oil until soft and browned, lose their bite and are transformed into something almost sweet. The addition of leeks makes for a more subtle and slightly sweeter topping.

YIELD: **4 TO 6 SERVINGS**

ACTIVE TIME: **2 HOURS**

TOTAL TIME: **3 HOURS**

INGREDIENTS

1 STICK OF UNSALTED BUTTER

¼ CUP OLIVE OIL

1 YELLOW ONION, SLICED THIN

1 LARGE LEEK, WHITE AND LIGHT GREEN PARTS ONLY, SLICED THIN, AND RINSED WELL

1 TEASPOON ACTIVE DRY YEAST

1 CUP WATER (110° TO 115°F)

2-2½ CUPS ALL-PURPOSE FLOUR, PLUS MORE FOR DUSTING

1 TEASPOON KOSHER SALT

SEA SALT, FOR TOPPING

1 TEASPOON FRESHLY GROUND BLACK PEPPER, PLUS MORE FOR TOPPING

PARMESAN CHEESE, GRATED, FOR TOPPING

DIRECTIONS

1. In a 12-inch cast-iron skillet, add the butter and 2 tablespoons of oil and warm over medium-low heat. When the butter is melted, add the onion and leek slices. Increase the heat to medium-high and cook, while stirring, until the onion and leek start to soften, about 5 minutes. Reduce heat to low and allow to cook, stirring occasionally, until cooked down and browned, about 10 to 15 minutes. Set aside.

2. Proof the yeast by mixing it with the warm water. Let sit for 10 minutes until foamy.

3. Combine the flour, kosher salt, and pepper, and stir into the yeast mixture. Stir to combine well. The dough will be sticky. Transfer to a floured surface and knead the dough until it loses its stickiness, adding more flour as needed, about 10 minutes.

4. Coat the bottom and sides of a large mixing bowl (ceramic is best) with a tablespoon of the olive oil. Place the ball of dough in the bowl, cover loosely with plastic wrap, put it in a naturally warm, draft-free location, and let it rise until doubled in size, about 45 minutes to 1 hour.

5. Preheat the oven to 450°F.

Continued...

6. Put the remaining olive oil in the skillet, and press the dough into it. Top with the caramelized onion/leek mix. Season generously with sea salt and pepper, then with Parmesan cheese. Cover loosely with plastic wrap and let rise for about 20 minutes.

7. Remove the plastic wrap, put the skillet on the middle rack of the oven, and bake for 25 to 30 minutes, until golden brown. Remove from oven and let rest for 5 minutes before removing from skillet to cool further.

Spinach & Ricotta Calzone

YIELD: **4 TO 6 SERVINGS**

ACTIVE TIME: **1 HOUR**

TOTAL TIME: **2 HOURS**

This pizza "pie" is gooey with cheese and plenty of lovely green spinach. If you want to spice this up, try some red pepper flakes, either in the calzone or on the side.

INGREDIENTS

FOR THE FILLING

2 TABLESPOONS OLIVE OIL

3 GARLIC CLOVES, MINCED

1 TEASPOON RED PEPPER FLAKES (OPTIONAL)

1 LB. FROZEN CHOPPED SPINACH
SALT AND PEPPER, TO TASTE

2 CUPS FRESH RICOTTA CHEESE

1 EGG, LIGHTLY BEATEN

½ CUP GRATED PARMESAN CHEESE

FOR THE DOUGH

1½ CUPS WATER (110° TO 115°F)

2 TEASPOONS ACTIVE DRY YEAST

4 CUPS ALL-PURPOSE FLOUR, PLUS MORE FOR DUSTING

2 TEASPOONS SALT

DIRECTIONS

1. To make the filling, place the olive oil, garlic, and red pepper flakes, if using, in a 12-inch cast-iron skillet over medium-high heat. Add the frozen spinach. Cook, while stirring, until the spinach is completely thawed, about 5 minutes.

2. Reduce heat to medium-low and cover, stirring occasionally, until the spinach is cooked through, another 15 minutes. Season with salt and pepper. Set aside but do not refrigerate. In a bowl, mix together the ricotta, egg, and Parmesan cheese.

3. To make the dough, combine the warm water and yeast in a large bowl, stirring to dissolve the yeast. When the mixture starts to foam, stir in the flour and salt and mix until the dough is just combined. It will be sticky.

4. Turn the dough out on a floured surface and start kneading until the flour is incorporated, adding more if necessary to make the dough malleable and smooth but not overdone.

5. Lightly grease a bowl and put the dough in it. Allow to rise while you prepare the filling and preheat the oven, about 30 minutes.

6. Preheat the oven to 400°F.

Continued...

7. On a lightly floured surface, turn out the dough and separate it into two equal pieces. Roll each piece into a 12-inch circle.

8. Place one circle in the skillet. The dough should extend about halfway up the side. Spread the cooked spinach mixture evenly over the dough, then dollop with the ricotta mixture. Use a spatula or the back of a large spoon to distribute the ricotta mixture. Place the other dough circle over the filling and crimp to seal the edges together with your fingers. Cut 4 slits in the top.

9. Bake for 25 minutes, until the crust is a lovely golden brown. Use pot holders or oven mitts to remove the skillet. Allow to cool for about 10 minutes before slicing and serving.

Pepperoni Bread

This is a favorite during football season, since the game hasn't actually started until this makes an appearance in front of the TV. Start in the morning for an afternoon game, as the dough needs to rise several times.

YIELD: **6 TO 8 SERVINGS**

ACTIVE TIME: **1 HOUR**

TOTAL TIME: **3 HOURS**

INGREDIENTS

1½ TEASPOONS ACTIVE DRY YEAST

1¼ CUPS WATER (110° TO 115°F)

1 TABLESPOON SUGAR

1½ TEASPOONS SALT, PLUS MORE TO TASTE

3½ CUPS ALL-PURPOSE FLOUR, PLUS MORE FOR DUSTING

PEPPER, TO TASTE

½ LB. PEPPERONI, SLIVERED

2 CUPS GRATED MOZZARELLA CHEESE

1 TEASPOON RED PEPPER FLAKES

1 TEASPOON DRIED OREGANO

1 TEASPOON GARLIC POWDER

1 TABLESPOON UNSALTED BUTTER, MELTED

DIRECTIONS

1. Proof the yeast by mixing it with the water and sugar in a large bowl and then stirring. Let sit until foamy, about 10 minutes. Add the salt and about half the flour to form a sticky dough. Cover the bowl with plastic wrap or a clean kitchen towel and let rise in a warm, draft-free place until it has doubled in size, about 1 hour.

2. Punch down the dough and add the remaining flour. Transfer to a floured surface and knead the dough until it's smooth and elastic, 8 to 10 minutes. Transfer to a lightly greased bowl and let sit for about 15 minutes.

3. On the floured surface, roll the dough out into a rectangle about 14 x 16 inches. Sprinkle with salt and pepper, spread the pieces of pepperoni around the dough, then the cheese, and top with a sprinkling of hot pepper flakes, oregano, and garlic powder. Roll up so that the dough maintains its length and then slice the roll into 6 or 8 rounds.

4. Grease a 10-inch cast-iron skillet with the butter and place the rounds in it. Cover with a clean kitchen towel and let them rise for about 1 hour. Preheat the oven to 375°F.

5. Bake the pepperoni bread for about 30 minutes, until golden on top and bubbling in the center. Serve immediately.

VARIATION: It's easy to make this into a full-blown meat lover's bread. In addition to the pepperoni, add about ¼ to ½ cup of any or each of diced pancetta, diced smoked ham, crumbled cooked bacon, sautéed sausage, or diced cooked meatballs.

Pizza Dough

YIELD: **2 BALLS OF DOUGH**

ACTIVE TIME: **30 MINUTES**

TOTAL TIME: **1 HOUR**

With this super-easy recipe, you can create amazing pizzas that can be personalized with almost anything you have in the refrigerator or pantry, from traditional cheese to "gourmet." And while the flavor will become more complex and the crust crispier if you allow the dough to rise for a couple of hours (or up to 3 days in the refrigerator), you can also roll it out and bake it within 15 minutes of making it.

INGREDIENTS

¾ CUP WATER (110° TO 115°F)

1 TEASPOON ACTIVE DRY YEAST

2 CUPS ALL-PURPOSE FLOUR, PLUS MORE FOR DUSTING

1½ TEASPOONS SALT

1 TABLESPOON OLIVE OIL

DIRECTIONS

1. If you'll be making pizza within the hour, preheat the oven to 450°F.

2. In a large bowl, add the warm water and yeast, stirring to dissolve the yeast. When the mixture starts to foam, stir in the flour and salt and mix until the dough is just combined. It will be sticky.

3. Turn out on a floured surface and start kneading until the flour is incorporated, adding more if necessary to make the dough malleable and smooth but not overdone.

4. If cooking immediately, allow the dough to rest for 15 minutes. While it's doing so, put a 10-inch cast-iron skillet in the oven. Prepare the toppings for the pizza. If preparing ahead of time, place dough in the refrigerator for up to 3 days.

5. After 15 minutes, or when ready, put a piece of parchment paper under the dough. Start rolling and pushing it out to form a 9-inch round that will fit in the skillet. If it bounces back, let it rest before pushing or rolling it out again.

6. When the round is formed, remove the skillet from the oven. Add the olive oil and brush to distribute over the bottom. Transfer the dough to the skillet and add the toppings.

7. Bake for 12 to 15 minutes, until the crust starts to brown and the toppings are hot and bubbling. Remove and allow to cool for 5 minutes before lifting or sliding the pizza out and serving.

Classic Corn Bread

YIELD: **4 TO 6 SERVINGS**

ACTIVE TIME: **1 HOUR**

TOTAL TIME: **3 TO 4 HOURS**

If you're going to make bread in a cast-iron skillet, you have to make corn bread. In fact, many restaurants now serve corn bread right in a cast-iron pan.

INGREDIENTS

4 CUPS FINELY GROUND YELLOW CORNMEAL

¾ CUP SUGAR

1 TABLESPOON SALT

4 CUPS BOILING WATER

1 CUP ALL-PURPOSE FLOUR

1 TABLESPOON UNSALTED BUTTER, MELTED, PLUS 1 TEASPOON

2 EGGS, LIGHTLY BEATEN

2 TEASPOONS BAKING POWDER

1 TEASPOON BAKING SODA

1 CUP WHOLE MILK

DIRECTIONS

1. In a large bowl, combine the cornmeal, sugar, salt, and boiling water. Stir to combine and let sit for several hours in a cool, dark place or overnight in the refrigerator. Stir occasionally while the batter is resting.

2. When ready to make, preheat oven to 450°F.

3. Add flour, the 1 tablespoon of melted butter, eggs, baking powder, baking soda, and milk to the batter. Stir to thoroughly combine.

4. Heat the skillet over medium-high heat and melt the teaspoon of butter in it. Add the batter.

5. Transfer the skillet to the oven and cook for 15 minutes.

6. Reduce the heat to 250°F and cook another 40 minutes, or until the bread is golden brown on top and set in the center.

Corn Tortillas

YIELD: **20 TORTILLAS**

ACTIVE TIME: **50 MINUTES**

TOTAL TIME: **50 MINUTES**

You really should be making your own corn tortillas, as a warm tortilla lifted straight from a cast-iron griddle or skillet is a thing of beauty. The main ingredient, masa harina, is a corn flour that is available in most grocery stores.

INGREDIENTS

2 CUPS MASA HARINA, PLUS MORE AS NEEDED

½ TEASPOON SALT

1 CUP WARM WATER (110°F), PLUS MORE AS NEEDED

2 TABLESPOONS VEGETABLE OIL OR MELTED LARD

DIRECTIONS

1. Place the masa harina and salt in a bowl and stir to combine. Slowly add the warm water and oil (or lard) and stir until they are incorporated and a soft dough forms. The dough should be quite soft and not at all sticky. If it is too dry, add more water. If the dough is too wet, add more masa harina.

2. Wrap the dough in plastic (or place it in a resealable bag) and let it rest at room temperature for 30 minutes. It can be stored in the refrigerator for up to 24 hours; just be careful not to let it dry out.

3. Cut a 16-inch piece of plastic wrap and lay half of it across the bottom plate of a tortilla press.

4. Place a large cast-iron griddle across two burners and warm over high heat.

5. Pinch off a small piece of the dough and roll it into a ball. Place in the center of the lined tortilla press, fold the plastic over the top of the dough, and press down the top plate to flatten the dough. Do not use too much force. If the tortilla is too thin, you will have a hard time getting it off of the plastic. Open the press and carefully peel off the disk of dough. Reset the plastic.

6. Place the disk on the hot, dry griddle and toast for 30 to 45 seconds. Flip over and cook for another minute. Remove from the griddle and set aside. Repeat the process with the remaining dough.

Pita Bread

YIELD: **16 PITAS**

ACTIVE TIME: **1 HOUR**

TOTAL TIME: **2 HOURS**

Pitas are delicious, somewhat chewy bread pockets that originated in the Mediterranean region. They can be filled with just about anything and are popular around the world, but are especially prevalent in Middle Eastern cuisine.

INGREDIENTS

1 PACKET OF ACTIVE DRY YEAST (2¼ TEASPOONS)

2½ CUPS WARM WATER (110° TO 115°F)

3 CUPS ALL-PURPOSE FLOUR, PLUS MORE FOR DUSTING

1 TABLESPOON OLIVE OIL, PLUS MORE FOR THE SKILLET

1 TABLESPOON SALT

3 CUPS WHOLE WHEAT FLOUR

UNSALTED BUTTER, FOR GREASING THE BOWL

DIRECTIONS

1. Proof the yeast by mixing with the warm water. Let sit for about 10 minutes until foamy.

2. In a large bowl, add the yeast mix into the all-purpose flour and stir until it forms a stiff dough. Cover and let the dough rise for about 1 hour.

3. Add the oil and salt to the dough and stir in the whole wheat flour in ½-cup increments. When finished, the dough should be soft. Turn onto a lightly floured surface and knead it until it is smooth and elastic, about 10 minutes.

4. Coat the bottom and sides of a large mixing bowl (ceramic is best) with butter. Place the ball of dough in the bowl, cover loosely with plastic wrap, put it in a naturally warm, draft-free location, and let it rise until doubled in size, about 45 minutes to 1 hour.

5. On a lightly floured surface, punch down the dough and cut into 16 pieces. Put the pieces on a baking sheet and cover with a kitchen towel while working with individual pieces.

6. Roll out the pieces with a rolling pin until they are approximately 7 inches across. Stack them between sheets of plastic wrap.

7. Warm a 10-inch cast-iron skillet over high heat and lightly oil the bottom. Cook the individual pitas for about 20 seconds on one side, then flip and cook for about a minute on the other side, until bubbles form. Turn again and continue to cook until the pita puffs up, another minute or so. Keep the skillet lightly oiled while cooking, and store the pitas on a plate under a clean kitchen towel until ready to serve.

Naan

YIELD: **8 PIECES**

ACTIVE TIME: **1 HOUR**

TOTAL TIME: **3 TO 4 HOURS**

*This is the bread that is traditionally served with Indian cuisine. It's usually cooked in a **tandoor** (clay oven) in India, but the cast-iron skillet works just fine.*

INGREDIENTS

1½ TEASPOONS ACTIVE DRY YEAST

½ TABLESPOON SUGAR

1 CUP WARM WATER (110° TO 115°F)

3 CUPS ALL-PURPOSE FLOUR OR 1½ CUPS ALL-PURPOSE AND 1½ CUPS WHOLE WHEAT PASTRY FLOUR, PLUS MORE FOR DUSTING

¼ TEASPOON SALT

1 TEASPOON BAKING POWDER

½ CUP PLAIN YOGURT

4 TABLESPOONS UNSALTED BUTTER, MELTED, PLUS MORE FOR GREASING THE BOWL

¼ CUP OLIVE OIL

DIRECTIONS

1. Proof the yeast by mixing it with the sugar and cup of the warm water. Let sit for 10 minutes until foamy.

2. In a bowl, add the remaining water, flour, salt, baking powder, and yeast mix. Stir to combine. Add the yogurt and 2 tablespoons of the butter and stir to form a soft dough.

3. Transfer to a lightly floured surface and knead the dough until it is springy and elastic, about 10 minutes.

4. Coat the bottom and sides of a large mixing bowl (ceramic is best) with butter. Place the ball of dough in the bowl, cover loosely with plastic wrap, put it in a naturally warm, draft-free location, and let it rise until doubled in size, about 1 to 2 hours.

5. Punch down the dough. Lightly flour a work surface again, take out the dough and, using a rolling pin, make a circle of it. Cut it into 8 slices (like a pie).

6. Heat the skillet over high heat until it is very hot, about 5 minutes. Working with individual pieces of dough, roll them out to soften the sharp edges and make the pieces look more like teardrops. Brush both sides with olive oil and, working one at a time, place the pieces in the skillet.

7. Cook for 1 minute, turn the dough with tongs, cover the skillet, and cook the other side for about a minute (no longer). Transfer cooked naan to a plate and cover with foil to keep warm while making the additional pieces. Serve warm.

TIP: You can add herbs or spices to the dough or the pan to make naan with different flavors, like adding chopped fresh parsley to the dough, or sprinkling the skillet lightly with cumin, coriander, or turmeric (or a combination) before cooking the pieces of naan. You can also use a seasoned olive oil to brush the pieces before cooking—one that has been infused with hot pepper flakes or roasted garlic.

CHAPTER 3

STARCHES

& SIDES

The recipes in this chapter show off just how delicious
carbs can be, and how well they play with others—and by others,
we don't just mean as a side dish for protein, we mean cast iron.
As you'll soon see, there's nothing better suited for a cast-iron
skillet than Stove-Top Potatoes (see page 69) and
Three-Cheese Mac & Cheese (see page 86).

Stove-Top Potatoes

YIELD: **4 TO 6 SERVINGS**

ACTIVE TIME: **5 MINUTES**

TOTAL TIME: **1 HOUR**

A classic side dish, made even better thanks to a little browning and crisping in a cast-iron pan. If you'd like to spice this up a little bit, try adding a pinch of cayenne pepper during the last 5 minutes of cooking.

INGREDIENTS

2½ LBS. RED OR FINGERLING POTATOES

2 TABLESPOONS OLIVE OIL

1 TEASPOON KOSHER SALT

PEPPER, TO TASTE

DIRECTIONS

1. If using red potatoes, cut them in half.

2. Place a 12-inch cast-iron skillet over medium-low heat for 5 minutes.

3. Place the potatoes, olive oil, salt, and pepper in a bowl and toss to coat.

4. Arrange the potatoes in a single layer in the skillet and cook for 10 minutes, while stirring occasionally.

5. Cover the pan, reduce the heat, and cook until the potatoes are fork-tender, about 30 minutes.

Potato Pancakes

YIELD: **6 SERVINGS**

ACTIVE TIME: **1 HOUR AND 30 MINUTES**

TOTAL TIME: **2 HOURS**

The key to great potato pancakes is getting as much liquid out of the grated potatoes as possible before adding them to the hot oil.

INGREDIENTS

6 LARGE RUSSET POTATOES, PEELED AND GRATED

1 LARGE ONION, GRATED

3 EGGS, BEATEN

¼ CUP BREADCRUMBS

SALT AND PEPPER, TO TASTE

1 CUP VEGETABLE OIL

DIRECTIONS

1. Squeeze as much liquid out of the potatoes as possible. Set aside half of the potatoes in a colander to drain. Take half of the potatoes, mix them with the onion, and process the mixture in a food processor or blender to create a rough puree. Don't overblend or chop, as the mix will get too starchy.

2. Put the puree in a separate colander to drain. Let both colanders drain for another 20 to 30 minutes. Push down on both to release more liquid and squeeze them again before continuing.

3. Combine the contents of the colanders in a large bowl. Add the eggs and breadcrumbs. Stir to thoroughly combine. Season with salt and pepper.

4. Heat a 12-inch cast-iron skillet over medium-high heat and add the oil. Take spoonfuls of the potato mix and place them in the oil. Cook for about 3 minutes per side. The pancakes should be golden brown on the outside and cooked through on the inside. You may need to adjust the heat to get the right cooking temperature, especially if you have more than three pancakes in the skillet at once.

5. Using a slotted spoon, transfer the cooked pancakes to a paper towel–lined plate. Keep warm until ready to serve.

Sweet Potato Pancakes

YIELD: **6 TO 8 SERVINGS**

ACTIVE TIME: **1 HOUR**

TOTAL TIME: **1 HOUR AND 30 MINUTES**

Sweet potatoes aren't as moist as russet potatoes, so you won't need as much draining time with them. These pancakes will probably not hold together as well as regular potato pancakes, but they are equally yummy and versatile. Serve with spinach and sour cream or refried beans, or put some on a baking sheet, top with grated cheddar, and broil for a couple of minutes to melt the cheese.

INGREDIENTS

6 LARGE SWEET POTATOES, PEELED AND GRATED

1 LARGE ONION, GRATED

3 EGGS, BEATEN

½ CUP MATZO MEAL

½ TEASPOON SUGAR

SALT AND PEPPER, TO TASTE

1 CUP VEGETABLE OIL

DIRECTIONS

1. Place the sweet potatoes in a colander and squeeze as much liquid out of the sweet potatoes as possible.

2. Combine the potatoes and onion and process in a food processor or blender to turn the vegetables into a rough puree. Don't overblend or chop, as the mix will get too starchy.

3. Squeeze the puree through a fine sieve to remove excess liquid, then let the mix sit and drain on its own for about 20 to 30 minutes.

4. Put the puree into a large bowl and add the eggs, matzo meal, and sugar. Stir to combine and season with salt and pepper.

5. Place a 12-inch cast-iron skillet over medium-high heat and add the oil. Take spoonfuls of the sweet potato mixture and place them in the oil. Cook for about 3 minutes per side. The pancakes should be golden brown on the outside and cooked through on the inside. You may need to adjust the heat to get the right cooking temperature, especially if you have more than three pancakes in the skillet at one time.

6. Use a slotted spoon to transfer the cooked pancakes to a paper towel–lined plate. Keep warm until ready to serve.

Crème Fraîche Potato Tart

The crème fraîche blankets very thin potato slices much like a traditional gratin.

YIELD: **4 TO 6 SERVINGS**

ACTIVE TIME: **45 MINUTES**

TOTAL TIME: **2 HOURS**

INGREDIENTS

1¼ CUPS CRÈME FRAÎCHE

1 TABLESPOON KOSHER SALT

½ TEASPOON BLACK PEPPER

PINCH OF GRATED NUTMEG

2 GARLIC CLOVES, CRUSHED

2 TEASPOONS CHOPPED
FRESH THYME

4 YUKON GOLD POTATOES,
PEELED AND SLICED VERY THIN

1 CUP DICED HAM (OPTIONAL)

ALL-PURPOSE FLOUR,
FOR DUSTING

2 FLAKY PASTRY CRUSTS
(SEE PAGE 214)

1 EGG YOLK

1 TABLESPOON HALF-AND-HALF

DIRECTIONS

1. Preheat the oven to 400°F.

2. In a bowl, add the crème fraîche, salt, pepper, nutmeg, garlic, and thyme. Stir to combine. Add the potato slices and ham, if using, and fold gently to cover with the crème.

3. On a lightly floured surface, roll out one crust so that it is just larger than the bottom of a 10-inch cast-iron skillet and lay it in the skillet.

4. Layer the potato slices in the crust, creating even, tight layers. Once all the potatoes are used up, use a rubber spatula to scrape the cream mixture into the skillet and distribute the mixture evenly.

5. On a lightly floured surface, roll out the top crust and crimp the edges with the bottom crust to seal. Blend the egg yolk with the half-and-half and brush the mixture over the top crust. Cut 4 to 5 slits in the middle.

6. Put the skillet in the oven and bake for 15 minutes. Reduce temperature to 350°F and continue to bake for 1 hour, or until potatoes are tender.

7. Serve hot or at room temperature.

Paprika-Spiked Potatoes

YIELD: **4 SERVINGS**

ACTIVE TIME: **45 MINUTES**

TOTAL TIME: **1 HOUR AND 15 MINUTES**

This smoky potato dish can be found in tapas bars all across Spain.

INGREDIENTS

4 MEDIUM POTATOES, CUT INTO THICK PIECES AND PARBOILED

1 ONION, WITH SKIN AND ROOT, HALVED

3 TABLESPOONS OLIVE OIL

2 CUPS WOOD CHIPS, SOAKED IN COLD WATER FOR 30 MINUTES

1 HEAD OF GARLIC, TOP ½ INCH REMOVED

1 (14 OZ.) CAN OF DICED TOMATOES, DRAINED

1 TABLESPOON SWEET PAPRIKA

1 TABLESPOON SHERRY VINEGAR

SALT, TO TASTE

SOUR CREAM, FOR SERVING

DIRECTIONS

1. Place the potatoes, onion, and 1 tablespoon of the olive oil in a mixing bowl and toss to coat.

2. Line a large cast-iron wok with foil, making sure that the foil extends over the side. Add the soaked wood chips and place the wok over medium heat.

3. When the wood chips are smoking heavily, place a wire rack above the wood chips and add the potatoes, onion, and garlic. Cover the wok with a lid, fold the foil over the lid to seal the wok as best you can, and smoke for 20 minutes. After 20 minutes, remove from the burner and keep the wok covered for another 20 minutes.

4. Meanwhile, to make salsa brava, combine the tomatoes, paprika, vinegar, and remaining olive oil in a blender and puree. Set the mixture aside.

5. Remove the garlic and onion from the smoker. Peel and roughly chop. Add to the mixture in the blender and puree until smooth. Season the salsa brava with salt. Serve the potatoes with sour cream and the salsa brava.

Rustic Potato Gratin

A testament to the brilliance of French cuisine, this layered dish has all the flavor in the world and is as simple as can be to make.

YIELD: **4 TO 6 SERVINGS**

ACTIVE TIME: **15 MINUTES**

TOTAL TIME: **45 MINUTES**

INGREDIENTS

4 GARLIC CLOVES, MINCED

LEAVES FROM 1 SMALL BUNCH OF PARSLEY, MINCED

2 TABLESPOONS MINCED FRESH THYME LEAVES

OLIVE OIL, TO TASTE

2 LBS. TOMATOES, SLICED ¼-INCH THICK

SALT AND PEPPER, TO TASTE

4 WAXY POTATOES, SLICED ¼-INCH THICK

CHICKEN STOCK (SEE PAGE 137), AS NEEDED

DIRECTIONS

1. Preheat your oven to 350°F.

2. Place the garlic, parsley, and thyme in a small bowl, stir to combine, and set it aside while you prepare the tomatoes.

3. Lightly oil a 12-inch cast-iron skillet or enameled cast-iron gratin dish and then add a layer of the tomato slices. Season with salt and pepper and add a layer of potatoes and a sprinkle of the garlic-and-parsley mixture. Drizzle with olive oil and continue the layering process until all of the tomatoes, potatoes, and garlic-and-parsley mixture have been used.

4. Cover with foil, place in the oven, and bake for 20 minutes. Remove from the oven and remove the foil. If tomatoes haven't released enough liquid to soften the potatoes, add a bit of the stock. Replace the foil and continue baking for 15 minutes.

5. Remove the foil, cook for an additional 5 minutes, and serve warm.

Zucchini Cakes with Sumac Yogurt

YIELD: **4 SERVINGS**

ACTIVE TIME: **15 MINUTES**

TOTAL TIME: **30 MINUTES**

Zucchini has a number of wonderful uses, and turning it into fritters is one of the easiest ways to get people excited about this summer squash. Staghorn sumac is native to the eastern United States, but its citric quality is massively underutilized outside of Middle Eastern cuisine. That is, until you try this recipe.

INGREDIENTS

1½ LBS. ZUCCHINI, GRATED

SALT AND PEPPER, TO TASTE

¼ CUP ALL-PURPOSE FLOUR

¼ CUP GRATED PARMESAN CHEESE

1 EGG, BEATEN

3 TABLESPOONS CANOLA OIL

1 CUP YOGURT

2 TEASPOONS FRESH LEMON JUICE

2 TABLESPOONS SUMAC POWDER

DIRECTIONS

1. Line a colander with cheesecloth and then place the grated zucchini in the colander, salt it, and let stand for 1 hour. Then press down to remove as much water from the zucchini as you can.

2. Place the zucchini, flour, Parmesan, and egg in a mixing bowl and stir to combine.

3. Use your hands to form handfuls of the mixture into balls and then gently press down on the balls to form them into patties.

4. Place the canola oil in a 12-inch cast-iron skillet and warm over medium-high heat.

5. Working in batches, place the patties into the oil, taking care not to crowd the skillet. Cook until golden brown, about 5 minutes. Flip them over and cook, until the fritters are also golden brown on that side, another 5 minutes. Remove from the skillet and drain on a paper towel–lined plate.

6. Place the yogurt, lemon juice, and sumac powder in a small bowl and stir to combine.

7. Season the patties with salt and pepper and serve the yogurt mixture on the side.

Poutine

YIELD: **4 TO 6 SERVINGS**

ACTIVE TIME: **35 MINUTES**

TOTAL TIME: **45 MINUTES**

A stone-cold Canadian classic that the recent celebration of comfort food has ushered into the mainstream. The joyful squeak provided by biting into the cheese curds is just one of the many pleasures available in this dish.

INGREDIENTS

4 CUPS VEGETABLE OIL

2 RUSSET POTATOES, CUT INTO STRIPS

SALT AND PEPPER, TO TASTE

4 TABLESPOONS UNSALTED BUTTER

¼ CUP ALL-PURPOSE FLOUR

1 GARLIC CLOVE, MINCED

4 CUPS BEEF STOCK (SEE RECIPE)

2 TABLESPOONS KETCHUP

1 TABLESPOON APPLE CIDER VINEGAR

½ TABLESPOON WORCESTERSHIRE SAUCE

2 CUPS CHEESE CURDS

BEEF STOCK

10 LBS. BEEF BONES

½ CUP VEGETABLE OIL

1 LEEK, TRIMMED, RINSED WELL, AND CUT INTO 1-INCH PIECES

1 LARGE YELLOW ONION, UNPEELED, ROOT CLEANED, CUT INTO 1-INCH PIECES

Continued...

DIRECTIONS

1. Place the vegetable oil in a large cast-iron Dutch oven and heat to 275°F. Add the potatoes and fry for 5 minutes, while stirring occasionally. Use a slotted spoon to remove the potatoes, transfer to a paper towel–lined plate, and let them cool completely.

2. Heat the oil to 350°F. Add the cooled potatoes and fry until golden brown, about 5 minutes. Transfer to a paper towel–lined plate and sprinkle with salt.

3. Place the butter in a saucepan and warm over medium-high heat. When it is melted, add the flour and cook, while stirring, until the mixture is smooth, about 2 minutes.

4. Add the garlic and cook until soft, about 2 minutes. Stir in the stock, ketchup, vinegar, and Worcestershire sauce, season with salt and pepper, and bring to a boil. Cook, while stirring, until the gravy has thickened, about 6 minutes.

5. Remove from heat and pour gravy over each serving of fries. Top each with a handful of the cheese curds and serve immediately.

BEEF STOCK

1. Preheat oven to 350°F. Lay the bones on a flat baking tray, place in oven, and cook until they are golden brown, 30 to 45 minutes. Remove and set aside.

2. Meanwhile, in a large stockpot, add the vegetable oil and warm over low heat. Add the vegetables and cook until the moisture has evaporated. This allows the flavor of the vegetables to become concentrated.

Continued...

2 LARGE CARROTS, PEELED AND
CUT INTO 1-INCH PIECES

1 CELERY STALK WITH LEAVES,
CUT INTO 1-INCH PIECES

10 QUARTS WATER

1 TEASPOON SALT

8 SPRIGS OF PARSLEY

5 SPRIGS OF THYME

2 BAY LEAVES

1 TEASPOON PEPPERCORNS

1 CUP TOMATO PASTE

3. Add the water, salt, bones, aromatics, and tomato paste to the stockpot, raise heat to high, and bring to a boil.

4. Reduce heat so that the stock simmers and cook for a minimum of 2 hours. Skim fat and impurities from the top as the stock cooks. As for when to stop cooking the stock, let the flavor be your guide.

5. When the stock is finished cooking, strain through a fine strainer or cheesecloth. Place stock in refrigerator to chill. Once cool, skim the fat layer from the top and discard. This will produce about 6 quarts and will keep in the freezer for about 6 months.

Bacon and Brown Sugar Baked Beans

YIELD: **6 TO 8 SERVINGS**

ACTIVE TIME: **30 MINUTES**

TOTAL TIME: **1½ TO 2 HOURS**

At times, using a cast-iron skillet makes you picture cowboys cooking over an open fire while their horses hang out behind them, and nothing is more quintessential to cast-iron cooking than baked beans. Baked beans are delicious and filling on their own, but they are the perfect accompaniment to grilled sausages, hot dogs, hamburgers, pork chops, or barbecued chicken.

INGREDIENTS

6 SLICES OF THICK-CUT BACON

½ ONION, DICED

½ CUP DICED BELL PEPPER

1 TEASPOON SALT, PLUS MORE TO TASTE

2 (14 OZ.) CANS OF PINTO BEANS, DRAINED AND RINSED

1 CUP BARBECUE SAUCE

1 TEASPOON DIJON MUSTARD

2 TABLESPOONS DARK BROWN SUGAR

FRESHLY GROUND BLACK PEPPER, TO TASTE

DIRECTIONS

1. Preheat the oven to 325°F.

2. Heat a 12-inch cast-iron skillet over medium heat and cook half of the bacon slices until just soft, about 8 minutes. Transfer to a paper towel–lined plate to drain.

3. Add the remaining slices of bacon, increase heat, and cook, flipping often, until browned. Reduce the heat to medium. Add the onion and bell pepper and cook, stirring occasionally, until the vegetables soften, another 8 minutes or so.

4. Add the salt, beans, barbecue sauce, mustard, and brown sugar. Stir, season with additional salt and a generous grind of fresh pepper, and leave on the stove until the sauce just starts to simmer.

5. Lay the partially cooked pieces of bacon on top of the beans and transfer the skillet to the oven.

6. Bake for 1 hour and check. The bacon should be crisp and browned, and the sauce should be thick. The dish can cook for another 15 to 30 minutes if the consistency isn't right. Be careful not to overcook, as the beans will start to dry out. An hour and 15 to 20 minutes is about right.

7. Remove from the oven and allow to cool slightly before serving.

Three-Cheese Mac & Cheese

YIELD: **6 SERVINGS**

ACTIVE TIME: **15 MINUTES**

TOTAL TIME: **1 HOUR**

The cheese in this dish will stick to your ribs. Reserve it for those nights when you're especially hungry and can afford to relax after the meal.

INGREDIENTS

SALT AND PEPPER, TO TASTE

½ LB. ELBOW MACARONI

7 TABLESPOONS UNSALTED BUTTER

2 CUPS BREAD CRUMBS (USE PANKO FOR AN EXTRA CRUNCHY TOP)

½ YELLOW ONION, MINCED

3 TABLESPOONS ALL-PURPOSE FLOUR

1 TABLESPOON YELLOW MUSTARD

1 TEASPOON TURMERIC

1 TEASPOON GRANULATED GARLIC

1 TEASPOON WHITE PEPPER

2 CUPS HALF-AND-HALF OR LIGHT CREAM

2 CUPS WHOLE MILK

1 LB. AMERICAN CHEESE, SLICED

10 OZ. BOURSIN CHEESE

1 LB. EXTRA SHARP CHEDDAR CHEESE, GRATED

DIRECTIONS

1. Preheat oven to 400°F.

2. Fill an enameled cast-iron Dutch oven with water and bring to a boil. Add some salt and then add the macaroni. Cook until slightly under al dente, about 6 to 7 minutes. Drain and set aside.

3. Place the pot over medium heat and add 3 tablespoons of the butter. Cook until the butter starts to give off a nutty smell and browns. Add the bread crumbs, stir, and cook until the bread crumbs start to look like wet sand, 4 to 5 minutes. Remove and set aside.

4. Wipe the Dutch oven out with a paper towel, place over medium-high heat, and add the onion and the remaining butter. Cook, while stirring, until the onion is translucent and soft, about 7 to 10 minutes. Add the flour and whisk until there are no lumps. Add the mustard, turmeric, granulated garlic, and white pepper and whisk until combined. Add the half-and-half or light cream and the milk and whisk until incorporated.

Continued...

5. Reduce heat to medium and bring the mixture to a simmer. Once you start to see small bubbles forming around the outside of the mixture, add the cheeses one at a time, whisking to combine before adding the next one. When all the cheese has been added and the mixture is smooth, cook until the flour taste is gone, 10 to 15 minutes. Return the pasta to the pot, stir, and top with the bread crumbs.

6. Place in the oven and bake for 10 to 15 minutes. Remove the pot from the oven and serve.

TIP: If you can't find Boursin, whisk some cream cheese and a little softened butter together.

Buttered Noodles with Cabbage

YIELD: **6 TO 8 SERVINGS**

ACTIVE TIME: **30 MINUTES**

TOTAL TIME: **2 HOURS AND 30 MINUTES**

A deceptive dish: it only has five ingredients, and yet it is the ultimate in comfort cooking. If you're committed to making it, know that the longer you cook the cabbage, the sweeter it becomes.

INGREDIENTS

1½ STICKS OF SALTED BUTTER, DIVIDED INTO TABLESPOONS

2 HEADS OF GREEN CABBAGE, CORED AND SLICED AS THIN AS POSSIBLE

SALT AND WHITE PEPPER, TO TASTE

1 LB. WIDE EGG NOODLES

DIRECTIONS

1. Place half of the butter in a large enameled cast-iron Dutch oven and melt it over medium heat.

2. Add the cabbage. If it doesn't fit initially, push down what does fit in the pot and add more as that wilts. Cover with a lid and cook for 10 minutes.

3. Remove the lid and add the remaining butter. Cover and cook for an additional 30 minutes, while stirring occasionally.

4. Reduce the heat to low and cook until the cabbage is extremely soft and browned, about 1 hour. Season with white pepper to taste.

5. About 20 minutes before the cabbage will be finished cooking, bring a pot of salted water to a boil. Place the egg noodles in the boiling water and cook until they are al dente, about 8 minutes. Drain, transfer to a large bowl, add the cabbage, and toss to combine. Serve immediately.

Polenta

YIELD: **4 TO 6 SERVINGS**

ACTIVE TIME: **30 MINUTES**

TOTAL TIME: **1 HOUR**

Polenta is cornmeal cooked into porridge and then baked or fried. It forms a lovely, bright yellow cake that is moist yet firm. It can be topped with all kinds of things, but in this recipe, it is the base for sautéed vegetables. Delicious!

INGREDIENTS

3 TABLESPOONS OLIVE OIL, PLUS MORE FOR THE SKILLET

1 CUP POLENTA

3 CUPS WATER

SALT AND PEPPER, TO TASTE

1 LB. BITTER GREENS (KALE, SWISS CHARD, ESCAROLE, OR DANDELION), STEMMED

3 GARLIC CLOVES, CHOPPED

RED PEPPER FLAKES, TO TASTE

ROMANO CHEESE, GRATED, FOR TOPPING

DIRECTIONS

1. Preheat the oven to 400°F.

2. Liberally oil a 12-inch cast-iron skillet and put it in the oven for a few minutes.

3. In a heavy saucepan, whisk together the polenta and water. Place over medium heat and bring to a boil, whisking to prevent lumps from forming. When bubbling, reduce the heat to low and simmer, uncovered, for a couple of minutes or until smooth. Season with salt and pepper.

4. Pour the polenta into the skillet. Put the skillet in the oven and bake for about 30 minutes, until the polenta is lightly golden and coming away from the edge of the pan.

5. While it's baking, make the greens. Bring a large pot of salted water to a boil, add the greens, and boil until very tender, 15 to 20 minutes. Drain in a colander and squeeze to remove excess moisture. Cut the greens into pieces. Heat the 3 tablespoons of olive oil in a pan, add the garlic, and cook, while stirring, until fragrant, about 2 minutes. Add the red pepper flakes, stir, and then add the greens. Cook until heated through. Season with salt and pepper. Keep warm until polenta is cooked.

6. Cut the polenta into wedges, top with greens, and sprinkle with Romano.

VARIATION: Substitute ½ lb. baby spinach leaves and ½ lb. kale (tough stems removed) for the 1 lb. of mixed greens.

Stuffing

YIELD: **10 SERVINGS**

ACTIVE TIME: **15 MINUTES**

TOTAL TIME: **1 HOUR AND 15 MINUTES**

Everyone knows that stuffing goes inside the bird, but if you are making that same recipe alongside the turkey, it is known as dressing. Follow whatever route you want with this preparation—it's delicious either way.

INGREDIENTS

1 STICK OF UNSALTED BUTTER

1 YELLOW ONION, CHOPPED

1 CUP CHOPPED CELERY

6 CUPS DAY-OLD BREAD CUBES

¾ TEASPOON DRIED THYME

SALT AND PEPPER, TO TASTE

3 CUPS CHICKEN STOCK
(SEE PAGE 137)

DIRECTIONS

1. Preheat the oven to 325°F.

2. Place the butter in a 10-inch cast-iron skillet and melt over medium heat. Pour out 2 tablespoons and reserve.

3. Add the onion and celery and cook, while stirring, until soft, about 6 minutes. Remove the pan from heat.

4. Place the bread cubes in a large bowl and stir in the cooked onion and celery. Add the thyme, season with salt and pepper, and stir to combine.

5. Add the broth and stir to incorporate. Let the mixture sit until the bread absorbs most of the broth.

6. Place the dressing in the cast-iron skillet and pour the reserved butter on top. Place in the oven and bake until browned, about 1 hour. Serve immediately.

CHAPTER 4

MEAT

———

Cast-iron cookware's celebrated ability to distribute and
hold heat truly shines when charged with a meat-based preparation,
effortlessly providing the crispy, seared exterior and juicy interior that
so many crave. Whether it's the mouthwatering Country Fried Steaks
and Gravy (see page 101), the fragrant Spicy Thai Flank Steak (see
page 113), or classic French bistro fare like the Steak au Poivre
(see page 97), this chapter offers something every carnivore
will be eager to sink their teeth into.

Steak au Poivre

YIELD: **2 SERVINGS**

ACTIVE TIME: **40 MINUTES**

TOTAL TIME: **2 HOURS**

When making this French classic, keep in mind that you'll get the best results from the best ingredients. Go farm-fresh for the meat, shallots, chives, and cream, if at all possible. Bon appétit!

INGREDIENTS

2 (8 OZ.) BONELESS STRIP STEAKS

KOSHER SALT, TO TASTE

1 TABLESPOON WHOLE BLACK PEPPERCORNS

1 TEASPOON VEGETABLE OIL

2 TABLESPOONS UNSALTED BUTTER, CUT INTO PIECES

2 SMALL SHALLOTS, MINCED

⅓ CUP COGNAC OR OTHER BRANDY

½ CUP HEAVY CREAM

SPRIGS OF ROSEMARY, FOR GARNISH (OPTIONAL)

DIRECTIONS

1. Preheat oven to 200°F.

2. Pat the steaks dry and season both sides with kosher salt.

3. Put the peppercorns in a sealed plastic bag and, working on a hard, flat surface, pound them with a meat tenderizer or mallet to crush them. Pour them onto a plate and press both sides of the steaks into them, distributing peppercorns evenly over the meat.

4. Place a 12-inch cast-iron skillet over medium-high heat for 5 minutes. Add the oil and swirl to coat the bottom of the pan. Put the steaks in the pan and sear on both sides, cooking for about 3 minutes a side for medium-rare.

5. Transfer steaks to a platter in the oven and keep warm as you make the sauce.

6. With the skillet over medium heat, add a tablespoon of the butter, let it melt, and add the shallots. As they sauté, stir up the bits stuck to the bottom of the pan. Cook until shallots are browned, about 3 minutes. Turn off the heat, pour the Cognac in the pan, swirl it around, and using a long-handled lighter, ignite it. The flame will subside in a minute or so. Turn the heat back on and cook the sauce until it is nearly boiling, while stirring constantly.

7. Add the cream and any juices from the platter the steaks are on. Reduce the heat and cook the sauce until somewhat reduced, about 5 minutes. Stir in the remaining tablespoon of butter.

8. Put the steaks on a plate and pour the sauce over them. Garnish with rosemary, if desired.

Seared Steak with Mushrooms and Potatoes

YIELD: **6 SERVINGS**

ACTIVE TIME: **30 MINUTES**

TOTAL TIME: **1 HOUR**

Once you get this recipe down, there's no reason to ever visit a fancy steak house again. For an added jolt of flavor, take whatever butter you have left over and mix it with some chopped thyme leaves. Place this on the steaks before serving and enjoy.

INGREDIENTS

2 TABLESPOONS KOSHER SALT OR COARSE SEA SALT

½ TEASPOON RED PEPPER FLAKES

½ TEASPOON WHOLE BLACK PEPPERCORNS

½ TEASPOON FENNEL SEEDS

½ TEASPOON MUSTARD SEEDS

½ TEASPOON CORIANDER SEEDS

6 (7 OZ.) STRIP STEAKS

2 LBS. FINGERLING POTATOES, HALVED LENGTHWISE

2 TABLESPOONS OLIVE OIL

1½ STICKS OF UNSALTED BUTTER, AT ROOM TEMPERATURE AND DIVIDED INTO 7 CHUNKS

6 SPRIGS OF THYME, PLUS 2 TABLESPOONS OF LEAVES FOR GARNISH

Continued...

DIRECTIONS

1. Preheat oven to 375°F.

2. Place the salt and red pepper flakes in a bowl. Use a spice grinder or a mortar and pestle to grind the peppercorns, fennel seeds, mustard seeds, and coriander seeds into a powder. Place the powder in the bowl with the salt and red pepper flakes and stir to combine.

3. Place steaks on a plate and season liberally with the seasoning blend. Set the steaks aside and let stand at room temperature for 1 hour.

4. Place the potatoes in a 12-inch cast-iron skillet and cover with water. Cook over high heat until the potatoes are tender but not mushy. Drain and set aside.

5. Wipe the skillet with a paper towel, add the olive oil, and warm over medium-high heat. Add the steaks to the pan, making sure you don't overcrowd. Cook steaks for 2 minutes, turn them over, and add 1 chunk of butter and 1 sprig of thyme for each steak. Cook steaks for 2 minutes, while spooning the butter over the steaks. Remove steaks and set aside. Remove thyme sprigs and discard.

Continued...

1 LARGE SHALLOT, MINCED

2 LBS. CREMINI MUSHROOMS, QUARTERED

1 LB. SHIITAKE MUSHROOMS, STEMMED AND SLICED THIN

1 LB. OYSTER MUSHROOMS, SLICED THIN

½ CUP CABERNET SAUVIGNON

¼ CUP WORCESTERSHIRE SAUCE

2 TABLESPOONS LIGHT TAMARI OR LIGHT SOY SAUCE

2 TABLESPOONS FISH SAUCE

6. Add the shallot and the remaining chunk of butter to the pan. Cook for 1 minute and add the cremini mushrooms. Cook for 5 minutes and then add the shiitake and oyster mushrooms. Cook for 3 more minutes and add the Cabernet Sauvignon. After 30 seconds, add the potatoes, Worcestershire sauce, tamari or soy sauce, and fish sauce. Stir until the mushrooms are evenly coated.

7. Return the steaks and their juices to the skillet. Place the skillet in the oven and cook until the steaks are warmed through, about 3 minutes.

8. Remove the skillet from the oven and slice the steaks at a 45° angle every 2 inches. Scoop the potatoes and vegetables onto a plate, top with the sliced steak, sprinkle with the fresh thyme leaves, and serve.

Country Fried Steaks and Gravy

YIELD: **2 SERVINGS**

ACTIVE TIME: **40 MINUTES**

TOTAL TIME: **2 HOURS**

Try your hand at one of the most iconic Southern inventions—Country Fried Steak! Be advised: high-quality ingredients will go a long way in this dish.

INGREDIENTS

2 (4 OZ.) ROUND STEAKS OR CUBE STEAKS

KOSHER SALT, TO TASTE

1 CUP ALL-PURPOSE FLOUR, PLUS 2 TABLESPOONS

½ TEASPOON FRESHLY GROUND BLACK PEPPER, PLUS MORE TO TASTE

1 CUP PEANUT, VEGETABLE, OR CANOLA OIL

2 TABLESPOONS UNSALTED BUTTER, CUT INTO PIECES

¾ CUP WHOLE MILK, PLUS MORE AS NEEDED

DIRECTIONS

1. Preheat oven to 200°F and place an ovenproof serving dish in it.

2. Prep steaks by patting them dry then seasoning both sides with kosher salt.

3. Add the cup of flour and ½ teaspoon of pepper to a shallow dish or bowl and dredge the steaks in it. Make sure they are evenly coated.

4. Place a 12-inch cast-iron skillet over medium-high heat for 5 minutes. Add the oil and the butter, coating the bottom of the pan. Put the steaks in the pan and fry on both sides, cooking for about 5 minutes a side.

5. Transfer steaks to the serving dish in the oven and keep warm as you make the gravy.

6. For the gravy, reduce the heat and pour out all but 2 tablespoons of the leftover pan drippings. Mix in the 2 tablespoons of flour, creating a roux. Continue to stir while turning the heat back up to medium.

7. Once the roux is smooth, slowly add the milk, stirring constantly until incorporated. If the gravy is too thick, add more milk. If too thin, continue to cook it until it reduces. Season with a sprinkle of salt and plenty of black pepper. Cover the steaks with the gravy and serve.

Argentine-Style Steak

If you are feeling adventurous and want this recipe to be truly authentic, ask your local butcher where to purchase some beef tallow. Serve this Argentinian dish with a simple salad of tomatoes, cucumbers, greens, and onions—you'll quickly fall in love with it.

YIELD: **4 SERVINGS**

ACTIVE TIME: **20 MINUTES**

TOTAL TIME: **24 HOURS**

INGREDIENTS

FOR THE CHIMICHURRI SAUCE

2 TABLESPOONS CHOPPED FRESH OREGANO

¼ CUP OLIVE OIL

2 CUPS CHOPPED FRESH PARSLEY

1½ CUPS CHOPPED CILANTRO LEAVES

1 SMALL WHITE OR YELLOW ONION, CHOPPED

2 SCALLIONS

1 JALAPEÑO PEPPER, SEEDED TO TASTE

¼ TABLESPOON SALT

¼ TABLESPOON PEPPER

¼ TABLESPOON ONION POWDER

¼ TABLESPOON GARLIC POWDER

1 TABLESPOON SUGAR

⅓ CUP WATER

Continued...

DIRECTIONS

1. To prepare the chimichurri sauce, place all of the ingredients in a blender and puree until smooth.

2. Transfer half of the sauce and the steaks to a container and let them marinate in the refrigerator overnight. Refrigerate the other half of the sauce in a separate container.

3. Preheat oven to 375°F.

4. Remove the steaks from the marinade and season both sides with salt. Set aside and let come to room temperature as you cook the potatoes and onions.

5. Place the white sweet potatoes, the Yukon Gold potatoes, and 1 tablespoon of salt in a 12-inch cast-iron skillet. Cover with water, bring to a boil, and cook until the potatoes are tender. Drain and set aside.

6. Wipe the pan with a paper towel, add the olive oil and beef tallow, and warm over medium-high heat. Add the steaks and cook for 2 minutes on each side. Remove the steaks from the pan and set aside.

Continued...

FOR THE STEAK, POTATOES & ONIONS

4 (5 TO 6 OZ.) NEW YORK
STRIP STEAKS

SALT AND PEPPER, TO TASTE

2 WHITE SWEET POTATOES, PEELED
AND DICED

2 YUKON GOLD POTATOES, PEELED
AND DICED

1 TABLESPOON OLIVE OIL

2 TABLESPOONS BEEF TALLOW

1 LARGE WHITE ONION,
SLICED THIN

¼ CUP WHITE VINEGAR OR
RED WINE VINEGAR

⅓ CUP DRY RED WINE (CABERNET
SAUVIGNON, TEMPRANILLO,
OR RIOJA)

1 TABLESPOON CHOPPED FRESH
OREGANO

7. Place the potatoes, onion, 3 tablespoons of chimichurri sauce, salt, and pepper in the pan and cook, while stirring, until the onion is cooked through, about 10 minutes. Add the vinegar, wine, and oregano and cook until the vinegar and wine have nearly evaporated, 5 minutes.

8. Return the steaks to the pan and place the skillet in the oven for 5 minutes.

9. Remove the pan from the oven, divide between serving plates, top with the remaining chimichurri sauce, and serve with a small salad.

TIP: Beef tallow is the rendered fat of beef, and it makes a great substitute for butter. If you can't find beef tallow at your local butcher, you can always ask for some beef fat, grind it in a food processor until fine, and cook it in a slow cooker for 6 to 8 hours. Then strain the fat through a coffee filter and store the liquid in the refrigerator until ready to use. To get 1 cup of tallow you'll need 1 lb. of beef fat.

Braised Short Ribs

YIELD: **4 SERVINGS**

ACTIVE TIME: **30 MINUTES**

TOTAL TIME: **3 HOURS AND 30 MINUTES**

This recipe is a twist on the New England classic—the Yankee pot roast. Short rib is an amazing cut from the brisket that benefits from cooking at low temperatures for a long time, which makes it the perfect candidate for low and slow cooking in a Dutch oven.

INGREDIENTS

2 TABLESPOONS CANOLA OIL

4 LBS. BONE-IN SHORT RIBS

SALT AND PEPPER, TO TASTE

2 LARGE ONIONS, SLICED

4 CARROTS, DICED

4 LARGE POTATOES, DICED

8 CUPS BEEF STOCK (SEE PAGE 82)

4 BAY LEAVES

2 SPRIGS OF ROSEMARY

2 SPRIGS OF THYME

½ CUP RED WINE

DIRECTIONS

1. Preheat the oven to 300°F.

2. Place the canola oil in a large skillet and warm it over medium-high heat. Pat the short ribs dry and season generously with salt.

3. Place the short ribs in the skillet and cook, while turning, until they are browned all over.

4. Transfer the browned short ribs to a Dutch oven with the onions, carrots, potatoes, stock, and bay leaves. Cover, place the Dutch oven in the oven, and cook until the short ribs are fork-tender and the meat easily comes away from the bone, about 3 to 4 hours.

5. Remove from the oven, strain through a fine sieve, and reserve the cooking liquid. Set the short ribs and vegetables aside.

6. Place the reserved liquid in a pan with the rosemary, thyme, and red wine. Cook over high heat until the sauce has reduced and started to thicken.

7. Season with salt and pepper. Divide the short ribs and vegetables between the serving plates and spoon 2 to 3 tablespoons of the sauce over each portion.

Classic Burgers

YIELD: **3 TO 4 BURGERS**

ACTIVE TIME: **30 MINUTES**

TOTAL TIME: **30 MINUTES**

A burger hot off the grill is a delicious thing. It's a staple of American dining. But if you want the best burger ever, you won't produce it on the grill. You'll make it in a cast-iron skillet. Why? Because the fat in the meat creates its own sauce, helping to brown and flavor the meat as it cooks. All of this drips off the grill. The cast iron holds the heat steady and hot, too, turning the surface of the burger the perfect, crispy dark brown from side to side. If your mouth is watering now, wait until you make these at home.

INGREDIENTS

1 LB. GROUND BEEF

VEGETABLE OIL, FOR THE SKILLET

SALT AND PEPPER, TO TASTE

HAMBURGER BUNS, FOR SERVING

SLICES OF CHEESE (OPTIONAL), FOR SERVING

SLICES OF COOKED BACON (OPTIONAL), FOR SERVING

LETTUCE, TOMATO, ONION (OPTIONAL), FOR SERVING

KETCHUP, MUSTARD, PICKLES, MAYONNAISE (OPTIONAL), FOR SERVING

DIRECTIONS

1. Refrigerate the ground beef until ready to use.

2. When it's time to make the burgers, brush a 12-inch cast-iron skillet with a thin sheen of oil, and heat it over medium-high heat. Don't overhandle the meat, simply take a handful of it (about 3 oz.) and form into a patty. Make 3 or 4, depending on how many will fit in the skillet.

3. Put the patties in the skillet and don't touch them. Let them start to cook over medium-high heat. Sprinkle some salt and pepper over them. Let them cook on one side for about 3 minutes.

4. When you flip the burgers, if you want cheese on one or all of them, put it on now.

5. Leave the burgers to cook on this side for 3 or 4 minutes. Scoop the burgers off the skillet with the spatula, slide each one onto a bun, top with whatever you like, and enjoy.

TIP: The kind of meat you use matters. The meat-to-fat ratio should be about 80:20. Most ground beef found in the grocery store is 85:15 or 90:10. If you have to go with one of these, choose the fattier proportion. The best thing to do, though, is ask the meat department to grind the meat for you. You want a chuck cut with a good amount of fat in it. The fat should show up as almost chunky in the meat, not pulverized.

Beef Stroganoff

YIELD: **4 TO 6 SERVINGS**

ACTIVE TIME: **40 MINUTES**

TOTAL TIME: **1 HOUR AND 30 MINUTES**

This dish is originally Russian and is made with pieces of beef served in a rich sauce that includes sour cream (smetana). It reportedly became popular in the mid-1800s. This is amazing on a cold winter day paired with a side of whole wheat bread and a cold cider.

INGREDIENTS

1 TABLESPOON OLIVE OIL, PLUS MORE AS NEEDED

1 LB. STEW BEEF, CUT INTO STRIPS

1 SMALL ONION, MINCED

2 GARLIC CLOVES, GRATED

½ CUP SLICED MUSHROOM CAPS

1½ CUPS BEEF STOCK (SEE PAGE 82)

¼ CUP DRY SHERRY

1 TABLESPOON WORCESTERSHIRE SAUCE

¼ CUP ALL-PURPOSE FLOUR

½ CUP SOUR CREAM

SALT AND PEPPER, TO TASTE

½ LB. EGG NOODLES, COOKED, FOR SERVING

DIRECTIONS

1. Heat the olive oil in a 12-inch cast-iron skillet over medium-high heat. Add the beef strips so they fit in the skillet (or work in batches). Fry them in the skillet, while turning so that all sides get browned, about 3 minutes. Transfer the beef pieces to a plate and cover with foil to keep warm.

2. Add a bit more oil if necessary, and sauté the onion, garlic, and mushrooms until soft, about 5 minutes. In the skillet, add the beef broth, sherry, and Worcestershire sauce. Bring to a boil, scraping the browned bits of meat and vegetables off the bottom of the pan. Put the flour in a bowl and add some of the heated sauce, using a whisk to form a paste. Add a bit more sauce to the bowl, and when the flour is fully incorporated, transfer all of it into the skillet and stir until incorporated. Continue to cook until the sauce thickens.

3. Reduce the heat and add the sour cream. Add the beef back to the skillet. When everything is hot, season with salt and pepper, and serve over the egg noodles.

YIELD: **4 TO 6 SERVINGS**

ACTIVE TIME: **10 MINUTES**

TOTAL TIME: **2 HOURS**

INGREDIENTS

3 LBS. SIRLOIN

6 TABLESPOONS OLIVE OIL

3 TABLESPOONS RED
WINE VINEGAR

JUICE OF 2 LEMONS

2 TEASPOONS CINNAMON

2 TABLESPOONS CORIANDER

1 TABLESPOON BLACK PEPPER

1 TEASPOON CARDAMOM

1 TEASPOON GROUND CLOVES

½ TEASPOON MACE

⅛ TEASPOON GROUND NUTMEG

1 TABLESPOON GARLIC POWDER

2 YELLOW ONIONS, SLICED INTO
THIN HALF-MOONS

SALT, TO TASTE

1 TEASPOON SUMAC POWDER

1 CUP PLAIN GREEK YOGURT,
FOR SERVING

PITA BREAD (SEE PAGE 64),
FOR SERVING

2 PERSIAN CUCUMBERS, DICED,
FOR SERVING

2 ROMA TOMATOES, DICED,
FOR SERVING

½ CUP FRESH MINT OR PARSLEY
LEAVES, TORN, FOR SERVING

Beef Shawarma

The secret to this dish is sumac, a popular spice in Middle Eastern cuisine that adds a beguiling sourness to dishes. This is typically served in a sandwich to be eaten on the go but is just as nice out on the patio with friends, a side of lemon rice, and a light cucumber salad.

DIRECTIONS

1. Place the meat in the freezer for 30 minutes so that it will be easier to slice. After 30 minutes, use an extremely sharp knife to slice it as thin as possible.

2. Place the sliced meat in a large mixing bowl. Add the olive oil, vinegar, lemon juice, cinnamon, coriander, pepper, cardamom, cloves, mace, nutmeg, and garlic powder and stir to combine. Place the meat in the refrigerator and let it marinate for 1 hour. If you have time, let the meat marinate overnight for even more flavor.

3. Place the sliced onions in a baking dish and cover with water. Add a pinch of salt and several ice cubes. Place in the refrigerator for at least 30 minutes and up to 4 hours.

4. Remove the meat from the refrigerator and let it come to room temperature. Drain the onions, squeeze them to remove any excess water, and place them in a bowl. Add the sumac powder and toss to coat. Set aside.

5. Warm a cast-iron grill pan over high heat. When it is warm, add the meat in batches and cook until it is browned all over.

6. To serve, place a dollop of yogurt on a pita and top with some of the meat, onions, cucumbers, tomatoes, and mint or parsley leaves.

Spicy Thai Flank Steak

YIELD: **4 SERVINGS**

ACTIVE TIME: **15 MINUTES**

TOTAL TIME: **30 MINUTES**

Theories abound as to why this is sometimes called Crying (or Weeping) Tiger, but all of them agree that it is delicious. You may also end up with tears in your eyes, overwhelmed by the good fortune of happening upon this dish.

INGREDIENTS

2 LBS. FLANK STEAK

2 TABLESPOONS SOY SAUCE

1 TABLESPOON OYSTER SAUCE

1 TABLESPOON BROWN SUGAR, PLUS 1 TEASPOON

1 LARGE TOMATO, SEEDED AND DICED

⅓ CUP FRESH LIME JUICE

¼ CUP FISH SAUCE (OPTIONAL)

2 TABLESPOONS MINCED CILANTRO LEAVES

1½ TABLESPOONS TOASTED RICE POWDER (SEE RECIPE)

1 TABLESPOON RED PEPPER FLAKES

1 CUP SOFT HERB LEAF MIX (MINT, THAI HOLY BASIL, AND CILANTRO), FOR GARNISH

1½ CUPS COOKED WHITE RICE, FOR SERVING

TOASTED RICE POWDER

½ CUP JASMINE RICE

DIRECTIONS

1. Pat the steak dry. Place it in a bowl and add the soy sauce, oyster sauce, and the 1 tablespoon of brown sugar. Stir to combine and then let the steak marinate for 10 minutes.

2. Place a cast-iron grill pan over high heat and spray it with nonstick cooking spray. Add the steak and cook on each side for 5 minutes for medium. Transfer to a plate, cover with foil, and let rest for 5 minutes before slicing into thin strips, making sure to cut across the grain.

3. To make the dipping sauce, place the tomato, lime juice, fish sauce (if using), remaining brown sugar, cilantro, Toasted Rice Powder, and red pepper flakes in a bowl and stir to combine. The powder won't dissolve, but it will lightly bind the rest of the ingredients together.

4. Divide the dipping sauce between the serving bowls. Top with the slices of beef, garnish with the soft herb leaf mix, and serve alongside the white rice.

TOASTED RICE POWDER

1. Heat a cast-iron skillet over medium-high heat. Add the rice and toast until browned.

2. Remove and grind into a fine powder with a mortar and pestle.

Goulash

YIELD: **6 TO 8 SERVINGS**

ACTIVE TIME: **30 MINUTES**

TOTAL TIME: **2 HOURS AND 30 MINUTES**

This rich and hearty dish tastes even better the next day. Redolent with the flavors of Eastern Europe—sweet paprika, earthy caraway, garlic, and sour cream—it is the comfort food you never knew you needed. Take your time making this; you will be rewarded.

INGREDIENTS

2 TABLESPOONS VEGETABLE OIL

3 LBS. BEEF CHUCK, TRIMMED

3 YELLOW ONIONS, CHOPPED

2 CARROTS, PEELED AND CHOPPED

2 BELL PEPPERS, SEEDED
AND CHOPPED

1 TEASPOON CARAWAY SEEDS

¼ CUP ALL-PURPOSE FLOUR

3 TABLESPOONS SWEET
HUNGARIAN PAPRIKA

3 TABLESPOONS TOMATO PASTE

2 GARLIC CLOVES, MINCED

1 TEASPOON SUGAR

SALT AND PEPPER, TO TASTE

2 CUPS BEEF STOCK (SEE PAGE 82)

1 LB. WIDE EGG NOODLES

1 CUP SOUR CREAM

DIRECTIONS

1. Place the oil in a large cast-iron Dutch oven and warm over medium heat. When the oil starts to smoke, add the meat in batches and cook until it is browned all over, taking care not to crowd the pot. Remove the browned meat and set aside.

2. Reduce the heat to medium-low. Wait 2 minutes and then add the onions, carrots, and peppers. Stir to coat with the pan drippings and sauté until the vegetables are golden brown, about 10 minutes. Add the caraway seeds, stir to incorporate, and cook until the seeds are fragrant, about 1 minute.

3. Add the flour, paprika, tomato paste, garlic, sugar, salt, and pepper and stir to incorporate. Add the broth and use a wooden spoon to scrape up any browned bits from the bottom of the pan.

4. Bring the goulash to a boil, reduce the heat, and let it simmer until it thickens slightly, about 10 minutes. Add the meat back to the Dutch oven, cover, and simmer over low heat until the meat is very tender, about 2 hours.

5. Approximately 20 minutes before the goulash will be done, bring water to a boil in a large pot. Add the egg noodles to the boiling water and cook until al dente. Drain and set aside.

6. To serve, stir in the sour cream and ladle the goulash over the cooked egg noodles.

Shepherd's Pie

YIELD: **4 TO 6 SERVINGS**

ACTIVE TIME: **45 MINUTES**

TOTAL TIME: **1 HOUR AND 30 MINUTES**

This "pie" doesn't have a crust. Instead, it has a top layer of mashed potatoes, which blankets the beef mixture and helps keep it juicy. In that sense, it works like a pie. Semantics aside, it's one of the best comfort foods you can make.

INGREDIENTS

6 RUSSET POTATOES, PEELED AND CUBED

½ TEASPOON SALT, PLUS MORE TO TASTE

1 STICK OF UNSALTED BUTTER, DIVIDED INTO TABLESPOONS

½ CUP WHOLE MILK PLAIN YOGURT, AS NEEDED

PEPPER, TO TASTE

1 TABLESPOON OLIVE OIL

½ YELLOW ONION, MINCED

1 LB. GROUND BEEF

1 (14 OZ.) CAN OF PETIT POIS (PEAS), DRAINED, OR 2 CUPS HIGH-QUALITY FROZEN PEAS

½ (14 OZ.) CAN OF CORN, DRAINED (OPTIONAL)

DIRECTIONS

1. Preheat the oven to 350°F.

2. Put the potato pieces in a large saucepan or pot and cover with cold water. Add the salt. Bring the water to a boil, reduce to a simmer, and cook the potatoes until soft, about 20 minutes. When they can be easily pierced with a sharp knife, they're cooked.

3. Drain the potato pieces and put them in a large bowl. Add 6 tablespoons of the butter and the milk and use a potato masher to make the mashed potatoes. If the mashed potatoes are too soupy, add yogurt in 1-tablespoon increments until they are creamy. Season with salt and pepper and set aside.

4. Place a 12-inch cast-iron skillet over medium heat, add the olive oil and onion, and cook until the onion is just soft, about 2 minutes. Add the ground beef and stir to break apart while it browns. When there is just a little pink left in the meat, drain the fat from the skillet. Stir in the peas and, if desired, the corn. Season with salt and pepper.

5. Spread the mashed potatoes over the meat and vegetables, distributing the potatoes evenly and smoothing the top. Cut the remaining 2 tablespoons of butter into slivers and dot the potatoes with them.

6. Cover with foil and bake for 30 minutes. Remove the foil and cook another 10 minutes until the potatoes are just browned.

7. Allow to cool for 5 minutes before serving.

Swedish Meatballs

YIELD: **4 TO 6 SERVINGS**

ACTIVE TIME: **1 HOUR**

TOTAL TIME: **1 HOUR AND 20 MINUTES**

This is excellent with a side of buttered noodles or boiled and buttered new potatoes seasoned with dill, basil, or parsley. You can also serve it as an appetizer at an intimate gathering, paired with lingonberry jam or red currant jelly.

INGREDIENTS

5 SLICES OF WHITE SANDWICH BREAD, CRUSTS REMOVED

¾ CUP WHOLE MILK

1½ LBS. GROUND BEEF

¾ LB. GROUND PORK

¼ LB. GROUND VEAL (OPTIONAL)

2 LARGE EGGS

2 TEASPOONS KOSHER SALT, PLUS MORE TO TASTE

1 TEASPOON NUTMEG

1 TEASPOON ALLSPICE

1 TEASPOON WHITE PEPPER

1 STICK OF UNSALTED BUTTER

1 SMALL YELLOW ONION, MINCED

¼ CUP ALL-PURPOSE FLOUR

4 CUPS BEEF STOCK (SEE PAGE 82), AT ROOM TEMPERATURE

½ CUP SOUR CREAM OR CRÈME FRAÎCHE

LINGONBERRY JAM OR RED CURRANT JELLY, FOR SERVING

DIRECTIONS

1. Tear the slices of bread into strips and place them in a bowl with the milk. Let the bread soak.

2. Place the meats, eggs, salt, nutmeg, allspice, and white pepper in a large bowl and use a wooden spoon or your hands to combine.

3. Remove the bread from the milk and squeeze to remove any excess liquid. Tear the bread into small pieces and stir into the meat mixture.

4. Place 2 tablespoons of the butter in a large cast-iron Dutch oven and melt over medium heat. Add the onion and sauté until it is translucent. Add the onion to the meat mixture and stir to combine.

5. Form the meat mixture into balls that are each about the size of a golf ball.

6. Place the remaining butter in a 12-inch cast-iron skillet and melt over medium heat. Working in batches, add the meatballs to the skillet and cook, while turning frequently, until they are browned all over. Use a slotted spoon to remove the browned meatballs and set them aside.

7. Sprinkle the flour into the skillet and stir to incorporate. Add the stock 2 tablespoons at a time, while stirring, until it is emulsified. You should have a thick gravy in the skillet when all of the stock has been incorporated.

Continued...

8. Return the meatballs to the skillet, gently stir to coat with the sauce, and reduce the heat to low. Cover the pan and simmer for 10 minutes.

9. Stir in the sour cream or crème fraîche and serve with lingonberry jam or red currant jelly.

Veal Scallopini

YIELD: **4 SERVINGS**

ACTIVE TIME: **15 MINUTES**

TOTAL TIME: **20 MINUTES**

This is an unexpected Italian preparation. The veal will get slightly crispy, exactly what you want alongside the meaty olives and vibrant lemon juice. If you don't eat veal, try this with chicken.

INGREDIENTS

½ CUP ALL-PURPOSE FLOUR

½ TEASPOON NUTMEG

SALT AND PEPPER, TO TASTE

2 TABLESPOONS UNSALTED BUTTER

1 LB. VEAL CUTLETS (ABOUT 4), POUNDED THIN

½ CUP BEEF STOCK (SEE PAGE 82)

¼ CUP SLICED GREEN OLIVES

ZEST AND JUICE OF 1 LEMON

DIRECTIONS

1. Warm a 12-inch cast-iron skillet over medium heat for 5 minutes.

2. Place the flour, nutmeg, salt, and pepper on a large plate and stir to combine.

3. Place the butter in the pan. When it is sizzling, dredge the veal in the seasoned flour until the scallops are coated lightly on both sides. Working in batches, place the veal in the skillet and cook for about 1 minute on each side, until it is browned and the juices run clear. Set the cooked veal aside.

4. Deglaze the pan with the stock. Add the olives, lemon zest, and lemon juice, stir to combine, and cook until heated through.

5. To serve, plate the veal and pour the pan sauce over each cutlet.

Lamb Stew

YIELD: **4 SERVINGS**

ACTIVE TIME: **30 MINUTES**

TOTAL TIME: **2 HOURS AND 30 MINUTES**

No food in this world can warm your soul more than this hearty, Old World–style stew, containing tender lamb and root vegetables. Toast some thick slices of sourdough bread to serve alongside, and you've got the ideal antidote for a winter day.

INGREDIENTS

2 LBS. BONELESS LAMB SHOULDER, CUT INTO BITE-SIZED CUBES

2 BAY LEAVES

6 YUKON GOLD POTATOES, SLICED ¼-INCH THICK

3 YELLOW ONIONS, SLICED

2 LARGE RUTABAGAS, PEELED AND SLICED ¼-INCH THICK

SALT AND PEPPER, TO TASTE

4 SPRIGS OF PARSLEY

2 LARGE CARROTS, PEELED AND SLICED ½-INCH THICK

DIRECTIONS

1. Place the lamb and bay leaves in a large cast-iron Dutch oven and cover with cold water. Bring to a boil over high heat and cook for 5 minutes. Remove the lamb with a slotted spoon and set aside. Transfer the broth and bay leaves to a separate container.

2. Place half of the potatoes in a layer at the bottom of the Dutch oven. Top with a layer of half of the onions and another layer consisting of half of the rutabagas. Add the lamb, season with salt and pepper, and top with layers of the remaining potatoes, onions, and rutabagas. Add the broth and bay leaves and bring to a boil. Reduce heat so that the stew simmers, cover, and cook for 1 hour.

3. Remove the lid, add the parsley and carrots, and simmer for another hour.

4. Remove the parsley and bay leaves and ladle the stew into warmed bowls.

Bacon-Wrapped Meatloaf

YIELD: 4 TO 6 SERVINGS

ACTIVE TIME: 10 MINUTES

TOTAL TIME: 1 HOUR

What kind of cookbook would this be without a take on this all-American darling? It's a standard in most homes because it's good enough to eat every single day.

INGREDIENTS

1½ LBS. GROUND BEEF

½ CUP GROUND PORK

1 YELLOW ONION, MINCED

2 TEASPOONS GARLIC POWDER

1 CUP BREAD CRUMBS

¼ CUP WHOLE MILK

2 EGGS, CRACKED AND LIGHTLY BEATEN

2 TABLESPOONS TOMATO PASTE

2 TABLESPOONS WORCESTERSHIRE SAUCE

2 TEASPOONS VEGETABLE OIL

8 SLICES OF BACON

DIRECTIONS

1. Preheat the oven to 375°F.

2. Place the beef, pork, onion, garlic powder, bread crumbs, milk, eggs, tomato paste, and Worcestershire sauce in a bowl and use a large spoon or your hands to combine.

3. Coat a 10-inch cast-iron skillet with vegetable oil. Place the meat mixture in the pan and form it into a dome. Place 4 slices of bacon over the top and place the other 4 on top in the opposite direction, weaving them together.

4. Place the skillet in the oven and bake for 45 minutes. Remove and let cool for 10 minutes before slicing into wedges.

CHAPTER 5

POULTRY

Cheap, lean, and versatile, one can never have too
many chicken-based recipes in their repertoire. But chicken is
far from the only fowl on the block, and it's worth mixing things up
with some turkey or duck. Rest assured, it all works wonderfully with
cast iron, which provides the crispy skin and juicy inside that so often
proves evasive when using other cookware. It's also wonderful for
braising, which is how you get the delectable, falling-off-
the-bone texture that makes dishes like Braised
Chicken Legs (see page 145).

Hot Wings

YIELD: **4 SERVINGS**

ACTIVE TIME: **30 MINUTES**

TOTAL TIME: **45 MINUTES**

The classic we've all come to know and love, now in the comfort of your home. This recipe can easily be altered, so don't hesitate to tinker and don't be bashful about tripling it if the gang is coming over.

INGREDIENTS

4 TABLESPOONS UNSALTED BUTTER

1 TABLESPOON WHITE VINEGAR

¾ CUP HOT SAUCE (TABASCO™ OR FRANK'S REDHOT® RECOMMENDED)

1 TEASPOON CAYENNE PEPPER (OPTIONAL)

6 CUPS VEGETABLE OIL

2 LBS. CHICKEN WINGS

1 CUP CORNSTARCH

SALT, TO TASTE

BLUE CHEESE DRESSING (SEE RECIPE), FOR SERVING

CELERY STICKS, FOR SERVING

BLUE CHEESE DRESSING

¼ CUP SOUR CREAM

¼ CUP MAYONNAISE

¼ CUP BUTTERMILK

1 TABLESPOON FRESH LEMON JUICE

PINCH OF BLACK PEPPER

1 CUP CRUMBLED BLUE CHEESE

DIRECTIONS

1. Place the butter in a large saucepan and warm over medium heat. When it has melted, whisk in the vinegar, hot sauce, and cayenne (if using), making sure not to breathe in the spicy steam. Remove the pan from the stove and cover to keep warm while you cook the wings.

2. Place the vegetable oil in a large enameled cast-iron Dutch oven and slowly bring it to 375°F over medium heat. This can take up to 10 minutes.

3. While the oil is heating, pat the wings dry and, working in batches, toss them in the cornstarch.

4. Add the coated wings to the oil in batches and fry until they are crispy, about 10 minutes. Transfer the fried chicken wings to a wire rack and season with salt.

5. Add the cooked wings to the spicy sauce in the saucepan. Remove them with a slotted spoon, arrange them on a platter, and serve them with the Blue Cheese Dressing and celery sticks.

BLUE CHEESE DRESSING

1. Place the sour cream, mayonnaise, buttermilk, lemon juice, and pepper in a bowl and whisk to combine.

2. Add the blue cheese and stir to incorporate. The dressing will keep in the refrigerator for up to 1 week.

Fried Chicken

YIELD: **4 SERVINGS**

ACTIVE TIME: **1 HOUR**

TOTAL TIME: **1 HOUR AND 30 MINUTES**

If you want the texture and flavor of deep-fried chicken without the mess, try this recipe. The cornflakes are essential!

INGREDIENTS

3 CHICKEN LEGS, SEPARATED INTO DRUMSTICKS AND THIGHS

¼ CUP ALL-PURPOSE FLOUR

SALT AND PEPPER, TO TASTE

1 CUP WHOLE MILK

1 TABLESPOON WHITE VINEGAR

2 EGGS, LIGHTLY BEATEN

1½ CUPS CORNFLAKES, FINELY CRUSHED

½ CUP PLAIN BREAD CRUMBS

1 TEASPOON PAPRIKA

1 CUP VEGETABLE OIL

DIRECTIONS

1. Preheat the oven to 400°F. Place a 12-inch cast-iron skillet in the oven to get it hot.

2. Rinse and dry the chicken pieces.

3. In a shallow bowl or cake pan, whisk together the flour with some salt and pepper. Combine the milk and the vinegar and let the combination sit for 10 minutes to create buttermilk. When ready, place the buttermilk in a bowl with the beaten eggs. In another large bowl, combine the cornflakes, bread crumbs, paprika, and 2 tablespoons of the vegetable oil.

4. Coat the chicken pieces one at a time by dipping each in the flour, then the buttermilk mixture, then the crumb mixture, being sure to coat all sides. When coated, put the pieces on a plate, cover with plastic wrap, and refrigerate for about 15 minutes.

5. Wearing oven mitts, carefully take the skillet out of the oven and put the remaining oil in it. Warm on low until hot. Add the cold chicken pieces and turn in the hot oil until both sides are coated.

6. Put the skillet back in the oven and bake for about 30 minutes, turning the pieces after 15 minutes. The chicken is done when the juices run clear when pierced with a knife. Serve immediately.

General Tso Chicken

YIELD: 4 SERVINGS

ACTIVE TIME: 1 HOUR AND 30 MINUTES

TOTAL TIME: 2 HOURS

You'll never find yourself reaching for the takeout menu again after whipping up this Chinese food favorite in a cast-iron skillet.

INGREDIENTS

1 EGG WHITE

1½ TEASPOONS TOASTED SESAME OIL

¼ CUP LOW-SODIUM SOY SAUCE, PLUS 1 TABLESPOON

¼ CUP CORNSTARCH, PLUS 1 TABLESPOON

1 LB. SKINLESS, BONELESS CHICKEN THIGHS, CUT INTO BITE-SIZED PIECES

1 TABLESPOON VEGETABLE OIL, PLUS MORE FOR FRYING

2 TABLESPOONS MINCED GINGER

3 GARLIC CLOVES, MINCED

1 CUP CHICKEN STOCK (SEE PAGE 136)

2 TEASPOONS SRIRACHA

3 TABLESPOONS SUGAR

3 SCALLIONS, SLICED THIN

DIRECTIONS

1. Place the egg white in a mixing bowl. Add the sesame oil, 1 tablespoon of soy sauce, and ¼ cup cornstarch. Whisk to combine. Add the chicken pieces and marinate at room temperature for about 30 minutes.

2. In a small saucepan, heat the tablespoon of oil over medium-high heat. Add the ginger and garlic and stir for about a minute. Add in the broth, Sriracha, sugar, remaining soy sauce, and tablespoon of cornstarch, and whisk to combine the ingredients. Continue to whisk until the sauce gets thick and glossy. Reduce the heat to low and cover to keep it warm.

3. Place a 10-inch cast-iron skillet over medium-high heat and add about ½ inch of vegetable oil. When hot, add the chicken one piece at a time so it doesn't splatter too much. Turn the pieces with a slotted spoon so that they brown on all sides. Cook until crispy, about 5 minutes. When the pieces are cooked, transfer them to a paper towel–lined plate to drain.

4. When all the pieces are cooked, stir them into the sauce with the scallions. Serve hot.

Chicken Kebabs

YIELD: **4 TO 6 SERVINGS**

ACTIVE TIME: **20 MINUTES**

TOTAL TIME: **2 TO 24 HOURS**

Once again, cast iron takes on a preparation that is universally associated with the grill and shows that it is more deserving of the job.

INGREDIENTS

2 TABLESPOONS PAPRIKA

1 TEASPOON TURMERIC

1 TEASPOON ONION POWDER

1 TEASPOON GARLIC POWDER

1 TABLESPOON DRIED OREGANO

¼ CUP OLIVE OIL, PLUS MORE AS NEEDED

2 TABLESPOONS WHITE WINE VINEGAR

1 CUP PLAIN GREEK YOGURT

1 TEASPOON KOSHER SALT, PLUS MORE TO TASTE

3 LBS. BONELESS, SKINLESS CHICKEN THIGHS, CUT INTO BITE-SIZED PIECES

BLACK PEPPER, TO TASTE

2 LEMONS, CUT INTO WEDGES, FOR SERVING

DIRECTIONS

1. Place the paprika, turmeric, onion powder, garlic powder, oregano, olive oil, vinegar, yogurt, and salt in a large bowl and whisk to combine.

2. Add the chicken pieces and stir until they are coated. Cover the bowl and let them marinate for at least 2 hours. If you have time, you can also let the chicken marinate overnight.

3. Place a cast-iron grill pan over medium-high heat and warm for 10 minutes.

4. While the pan is heating up, thread the chicken onto skewers and season with salt and pepper.

5. Brush the grill pan with a light coating of olive oil and then add the chicken kebabs. Cook, while turning occasionally, until the chicken is golden brown and cooked through, approximately 10 minutes.

6. Serve warm or at room temperature with the lemon wedges.

Turkey Chili

YIELD: **6 TO 8 SERVINGS**

ACTIVE TIME: **35 MINUTES**

TOTAL TIME: **2 HOURS AND 35 MINUTES**

While chili isn't always the first use for leftover turkey, this spicy combination is sure to make a lasting impression.

INGREDIENTS

1 TABLESPOON OLIVE OIL

1 YELLOW ONION, DICED

5 GARLIC CLOVES, MINCED

1 TABLESPOON CHOPPED
FRESH OREGANO

BLACK PEPPER, TO TASTE

1 TABLESPOON CUMIN

2 TEASPOONS CHILI POWDER

2 CUPS CHICKEN STOCK
(SEE RECIPE)

½ LB. TOMATOES (CANNED
OR FRESH)

3 DRIED RED NEW MEXICO CHILIES

1 RED BELL PEPPER, SEEDED
AND DICED

PINCH OF SALT

1 (14 OZ.) CAN OF CHICKPEAS

1 LB. LEFTOVER TURKEY

Continued...

DIRECTIONS

1. Place the olive oil in a cast-iron Dutch oven and warm over medium-high heat.

2. Add the onion, garlic, oregano, pepper, cumin, and chili powder. Cook for 5 minutes, stirring often.

3. Add the stock, tomatoes, dried chilies, bell pepper, salt, chickpeas, and turkey.

4. Stir the mixture, cover, and reduce the heat to low. Cook for 2 hours, stirring occasionally.

5. Scoop chili into bowls and top with cheese and sour cream, if desired. Serve with the Rosemary Butter and Classic Corn Bread.

ROSEMARY BUTTER

1. Place the butter, salt, and rosemary in a bowl and beat until light and fluffy.

2. Place the whipped butter in a container and refrigerate until needed.

CHICKEN STOCK

Yield: 3 quarts   Active Time: 10 Minutes
Total Time: 3 Hours and 30 Minutes

5 lbs. chicken bones, skin, and trimmings

4 celery ribs, cut into thick slices

2 onions, quartered

2 carrots, cut into thick slices

2 tablespoons whole black peppercorns

6 garlic cloves, peeled

4 sprigs parsley

4 sprigs thyme or 1 teaspoon dried

2 bay leaves

1. Place 6 quarts water and chicken in a large stockpot and bring to a boil over high heat. Reduce the heat to low and skim off foam that rises during the first 10 to 15 minutes of simmering. Simmer stock, uncovered, for 1 hour, then add remainder of the ingredients. Simmer for 2½ hours.

2. Strain stock through a fine-meshed sieve, pushing with the back of a spoon to extract as much liquid as possible. Discard solids, divide stock among small plastic containers and refrigerate or freeze if not using immediately.

2 CUPS SHREDDED CHEDDAR CHEESE (OPTIONAL)

1 CUP SOUR CREAM (OPTIONAL)

ROSEMARY BUTTER (SEE RECIPE), FOR SERVING

CLASSIC CORN BREAD (SEE PAGE 61), FOR SERVING

ROSEMARY BUTTER

4 TABLESPOONS UNSALTED BUTTER, AT ROOM TEMPERATURE

PINCH OF SALT

LEAVES FROM 2 SPRIGS OF ROSEMARY, MINCED

Chicken Stew

YIELD: **6 SERVINGS**

ACTIVE TIME: **15 TO 20 MINUTES**

TOTAL TIME: **1 HOUR AND 45 MINUTES**

A day's worth of protein, veggies, and flavor are packed into this stew—which requires minimal effort on your part.

INGREDIENTS

2 TABLESPOONS OLIVE OIL

2 LBS. CHICKEN THIGHS

SALT AND PEPPER, TO TASTE

1 WHITE ONION, DICED

3 CELERY STALKS, DICED

2 CARROTS, DICED

2 PARSNIPS, DICED

1 ZUCCHINI, DICED

1 YELLOW SQUASH, DICED

3 GARLIC CLOVES, MINCED

8 CUPS CHICKEN STOCK
(SEE PAGE 137)

2 BAY LEAVES

FRESH BASIL, CHOPPED,
FOR GARNISH (OPTIONAL)

DIRECTIONS

1. Place the olive oil in a cast-iron Dutch oven and warm over medium-high heat. Season the chicken thighs with salt and pepper and place them in the Dutch oven, skin side down. Cook for 5 minutes on each side. Remove and set aside.

2. Add the onion, celery, carrots, and parsnips to the pot and cook for 5 to 7 minutes, until the onion starts to get translucent. Season with a pinch of salt and pepper and then add the zucchini, squash, and garlic. Cook for 5 minutes, while stirring, until the garlic is fragrant.

3. Season with salt and pepper and add the chicken thighs, stock, and bay leaves. Reduce heat to medium, cover, and cook for 1 hour or until the chicken is falling off the bone. Season with salt and pepper to taste. Discard the bay leaves and, if desired, garnish with fresh basil before serving.

Chicken Pot Pie

When you have leftover chicken, reach for this recipe. Simply prepare the chicken mixture in the skillet, top with a crust, and bake for a delicious and satisfying meal.

YIELD: **4 TO 6 SERVINGS**

ACTIVE TIME: **1 HOUR**

TOTAL TIME: **2 HOURS**

INGREDIENTS

2 TABLESPOONS OLIVE OIL

½ YELLOW ONION, DICED

1 GARLIC CLOVE, CHOPPED

1 CARROT, PEELED AND CHOPPED

1¼ CUPS WHOLE MILK, AT ROOM TEMPERATURE

2 TABLESPOONS UNSALTED BUTTER, CUT INTO SMALLER SLICES

2 TABLESPOONS ALL-PURPOSE FLOUR, PLUS MORE FOR DUSTING

1½ CUPS COOKED CHICKEN, CUT INTO BITE-SIZED PIECES

¾ CUP CHOPPED FROZEN GREEN BEANS

SALT AND PEPPER, TO TASTE

½ TEASPOON CAYENNE PEPPER (OPTIONAL)

1 FLAKY PASTRY CRUST (SEE PAGE 215)

1 TABLESPOON HALF-AND-HALF

DIRECTIONS

1. Preheat the oven to 350°F.

2. In a small skillet other than the cast-iron skillet, heat the olive oil. Add the onion and garlic and cook, while stirring, for about 2 minutes. Add the carrot, reduce the heat to low, cover, and cook, while stirring occasionally, until the carrots start to soften and the onion caramelizes, about 5 minutes. Set aside.

3. Before starting to make the white sauce, be sure the milk is at room temperature. If it's not, microwave it so that it's just warm, about 15 to 20 seconds. Have the milk ready.

4. Place the butter in a 12-inch cast-iron skillet and melt over medium heat. Sprinkle the flour over it and stir quickly yet gently to blend. Reduce the heat slightly so the butter doesn't burn. Stir until the butter and flour form a soft paste.

5. Add just a little of the warm milk and stir constantly to blend it in. Add more milk in small increments, working after each addition to stir it into the flour-and-butter mixture smoothly. Work in this manner until all the milk has been incorporated. Continue to stir the sauce while cooking over low heat until it thickens, about 5 minutes.

6. Add the chicken pieces, green beans, and vegetable mixture from the other skillet. Season with salt and pepper. If you want a hint of heat, add the cayenne pepper.

Continued...

7. On a flour-dusted work surface, roll out the crust so it will fit over the filling. Lay it gently on top, push down slightly to secure, and cut 3 or 4 slits in the middle. Brush the crust with the half-and-half.

8. Put the skillet in the oven and bake for 30 to 40 minutes, until the crust is browned and the filling is bubbly.

9. Remove from the oven and let cool slightly before serving.

Chicken Fajitas

YIELD: **6 TO 8 SERVINGS**

ACTIVE TIME: **30 MINUTES**

TOTAL TIME: **5 HOURS**

The trick is to bring this dish to the table while the meat and veggies are still sizzling, so you'll want to be sure you have any sides prepped ahead of time. To start, you'll want tortillas, guacamole, salsa, sliced jalapeños, sliced black olives, and sour cream.

INGREDIENTS

FOR THE CHICKEN

½ CUP ORANGE JUICE

JUICE OF 1 LIME

4 GARLIC CLOVES, MINCED

1 JALAPEÑO PEPPER, SEEDED AND DICED

2 TABLESPOONS CHOPPED FRESH CILANTRO

1 TEASPOON CUMIN

1 TEASPOON DRIED OREGANO

SALT AND PEPPER, TO TASTE

3 TABLESPOONS OLIVE OIL

3-4 BONELESS, SKINLESS CHICKEN BREASTS, CUT INTO STRIPS

FOR THE VEGETABLES

2 TABLESPOONS OLIVE OIL

1 RED ONION, SLICED THIN

Continued...

DIRECTIONS

1. To prepare the chicken, place the orange juice, lime juice, garlic, jalapeño, cilantro, cumin, oregano, salt, and pepper in a bowl and stir. When thoroughly combined, add the olive oil. Put the chicken pieces in the mix, stir, cover with plastic wrap, and refrigerate for about 4 hours.

2. Place a 12-inch cast-iron skillet over medium-high heat. Remove the chicken from the marinade with a slotted spoon and put it in the skillet, stirring and turning the pieces so they brown on all sides. Cook thoroughly, about 8 to 10 minutes. Transfer the cooked chicken to a platter and cover loosely with foil.

3. To prepare the vegetables, reduce the heat to medium, add the oil, and then add the onion, peppers, and garlic. Cook, while stirring, until the vegetables soften, 3 to 5 minutes. Add the lime juice and cilantro and cook until the vegetables start to brown. Season with salt and pepper.

4. While the vegetables are still sizzling, push them to one side of the pan and put the chicken on the other side. Serve immediately.

VARIATION: You can use the same ingredients to make steak fajitas, but substitute 1 lb. of flank steak for the chicken and marinate it overnight. Don't slice the steak until it has been cooked.

1 RED BELL PEPPER, SEEDED
AND SLICED THIN

1 GREEN BELL PEPPER, SEEDED
AND SLICED THIN

1 YELLOW BELL PEPPER, SEEDED
AND SLICED THIN

2 JALAPEŃO OR SERRANO PEPPERS,
SEEDED AND SLICED THIN

3 GARLIC CLOVES, MINCED

¼ CUP FRESH LIME JUICE

½ CUP CHOPPED FRESH CILANTRO

SALT AND PEPPER, TO TASTE

Braised Chicken Legs

YIELD: **6 SERVINGS**

ACTIVE TIME: **30 MINUTES**

TOTAL TIME: **1 HOUR AND 10 MINUTES**

There's something so classic about these flavors that it's hard to resist the potato-and-fennel combo. This is a great comfort food for a cold day, as it's likely to stick with you for a while.

INGREDIENTS

⅓ CUP OLIVE OIL, PLUS 2 TABLESPOONS

6 CHICKEN LEGS

1 TABLESPOON KOSHER SALT

1 TABLESPOON CRACKED BLACK PEPPER

½ CUP MINCED SHALLOTS

2 GARLIC CLOVES, MINCED

2 RED POTATOES, DICED

3-4 YELLOW POTATOES, DICED

3 FENNEL BULBS, DICED (RESERVE THE FRONDS FOR GARNISH)

1 TEASPOON CELERY SEEDS

1 TEASPOON FENNEL SEEDS

½ CUP SUN-DRIED TOMATOES

1 CUP CHARDONNAY

6 TABLESPOONS SALTED BUTTER

DIRECTIONS

1. Place a cast-iron Dutch oven over medium-high heat and add the ⅓ cup of the olive oil. While the oil heats up, rub the chicken legs with the remaining oil and season with the salt and pepper. When the oil is hot, add half of the chicken, skin side down, and cook until the skin is golden brown and crusted. Remove, set aside, and repeat with the remaining chicken legs.

2. Preheat the oven to 400°F. Add the shallots and garlic to the Dutch oven and use a wooden spoon to scrape all of the browned bits from the bottom. Cook until the shallots and garlic darken, about 3 minutes.

3. Turn the heat up to high and add the remaining ingredients, save the Chardonnay and the butter. Cook for about 15 minutes, while stirring every few minutes.

4. Add the wine and the butter, stir, and then return the chicken to the pan, skin-side up. Reduce the heat, cover, and cook until the potatoes are soft and the chicken is 155°F in the center, about 20 minutes. Remove the lid, transfer the Dutch oven to the oven, and cook until the chicken is 165°F in the center, about 10 minutes.

TIP: To check the temperature of the chicken, insert a kitchen thermometer at the fattest point. Digital thermometers are pretty cheap, about $10 to $15 for the basic model. To calibrate the thermometer, submerge the probe in a cup of ice water; it should read 32°F.

Roasted Cornish Game Hens

YIELD: **4 SERVINGS**

ACTIVE TIME: **20 TO 30 MINUTES**

TOTAL TIME: **3 TO 9 HOURS**

There is something so elegant about everyone getting their own bird. Brining will help the hens retain moisture, and keep them from getting dry if you overcook them, so it is well worth the additional time.

INGREDIENTS

FOR THE BRINE (OPTIONAL)

5 CUPS WATER

1 CUP SUGAR

1 CUP SALT

2 BAY LEAVES

1 TABLESPOON CRACKED BLACK PEPPER

1 TABLESPOON CORIANDER SEEDS, GROUND

½ TABLESPOON FENNEL SEEDS, GROUND

½ TABLESPOON CELERY SEEDS, GROUND

FOR THE HENS

4 (3-LB.) CORNISH GAME HENS

1½ TABLESPOONS MINCED FRESH THYME

1½ TABLESPOONS MINCED FRESH SAGE

Continued...

DIRECTIONS

1. In a large stockpot, add the water, sugar, and salt and cook over medium-high heat until the sugar and salt dissolve. Add the remaining ingredients, remove from heat, and let cool to room temperature. Place the Cornish game hens in the brine, making sure they are completely covered, using a small bowl to weigh them down if necessary. Soak in the brine for 4 to 6 hours.

2. Preheat the oven to 375°F. Place the thyme, sage, rosemary, and minced garlic in a bowl and stir until combined.

3. Remove the Cornish game hens from the brine, pat dry, and rub with olive oil. Sprinkle with salt, pepper, and the herb-and-garlic mixture. Let the game hens stand at room temperature for approximately 30 minutes.

4. In a cast-iron Dutch oven, add 3 tablespoons of olive oil, the smashed garlic cloves, onion, and 1 tablespoon of salt. Cook over medium-high heat, reducing the heat if the onion starts to burn or dry out, until the onion is dark brown. Remove and set aside.

5. Place the Brussels sprouts, the remaining olive oil, and a pinch of salt in the Dutch oven. Stir until the brussels sprouts are evenly coated.

Continued...

1½ TABLESPOONS MINCED
FRESH ROSEMARY

11 GARLIC CLOVES, 3 MINCED,
8 SMASHED

5 TABLESPOONS OLIVE OIL, PLUS
MORE FOR RUBBING

SALT AND PEPPER, TO TASTE

1 LARGE WHITE ONION, SLICED

2 LBS. BABY BRUSSELS
SPROUTS, HALVED

1 LEMON, QUARTERED, PLUS ½ OF
A LEMON

4 TABLESPOONS UNSALTED BUTTER

6. Spread the Brussels sprouts into a layer in the Dutch oven, cover with a layer of the garlic-and-onion mixture, and place the Cornish hens in the Dutch oven, breast side up. Put the ½ of a lemon in the center of the Dutch oven. Place the lemon quarters against the edge of the Dutch oven and between each hen. Place the Dutch oven in the oven and cook for 30 to 40 minutes.

7. Raise the heat to 400°F, remove the Dutch oven from the oven, and spin each hen 180°. Rub the top of each with the butter, return the Dutch oven to the oven, and cook for 20 minutes, or until the internal temperature of each hen is 165°F. Remove the Dutch oven from the oven and let stand for up to 30 minutes before serving.

TIP: If you plan on removing and discarding the skin after the hens are cooked, try cooking them breast side down, as this will ensure that they are even juicier.

Chicken Thighs with Roasted Tomato Sauce

YIELD: **4 SERVINGS**

ACTIVE TIME: **25 MINUTES**

TOTAL TIME: **1 HOUR**

Boneless, skinless chicken makes prep a lot easier for many dishes, but you need both to stick around in this preparation. Searing the skin renders the fat and adds a tremendous amount of flavor, and cooking it on the bone ensures that the meat remains moist and tender.

INGREDIENTS

FOR THE CHICKEN THIGHS

2 TABLESPOONS OLIVE OIL

SALT AND PEPPER, TO TASTE

2 TEASPOONS PAPRIKA

2 TEASPOONS CUMIN

2 TEASPOONS GROUND
FENNEL SEEDS

4 CHICKEN THIGHS

1 CUP CHERRY TOMATOES

2 GARLIC CLOVES, CRUSHED

1 SHALLOT, SLICED

½ CUP WHITE WINE

FOR THE TABBOULEH

1 CUP BULGUR WHEAT

2 CUPS WATER

1 SHALLOT, HALVED

2 SPRIGS OF THYME

Continued...

DIRECTIONS

1. Preheat the oven to 450°F. Place the olive oil in a cast-iron skillet and warm over medium-high heat. Sprinkle salt, pepper, paprika, cumin, and ground fennel on the chicken thighs. When the oil starts to smoke, place the thighs skin side down in the pan and sear until brown.

2. Turn the thighs over and place the pan in the oven. Cook until the internal temperature is 165°F, about 16 minutes. Halfway through the cooking time, add the tomatoes, garlic, and shallot to the pan.

3. When the chicken is fully cooked, remove from the oven and transfer to a plate. Leave the vegetables in the pan, add the white wine, and place over high heat. Cook for 1 minute, while shaking the pan. Transfer the contents of the pan to a blender, puree until smooth, and season to taste. Set aside.

4. Prepare the tabbouleh. Place the bulgur, water, shallot, thyme, and salt in a saucepan and bring to a boil. Remove from heat, cover the pan with foil, and let sit until the bulgur has absorbed all the liquid. Fluff with a fork, remove the shallot and thyme, and add the remaining ingredients. Stir to combine and season with salt and pepper.

5. To serve, place some of the tabbouleh on each plate. Top with a chicken thigh and spoon some of the puree over it.

1 TABLESPOON SALT, PLUS MORE
TO TASTE

1 TABLESPOON CHOPPED
CILANTRO

1 TABLESPOON CHOPPED PARSLEY

2 TABLESPOONS CHOPPED
SCALLIONS

1½ TABLESPOONS FRESH
LIME JUICE

½ CUP DICED TOMATO

½ CUP DICED CUCUMBER

½ TEASPOON MINCED GARLIC

3 TABLESPOONS OLIVE OIL

PEPPER, TO TASTE

Korean Chicken Thighs with Sweet Potato Noodles

INGREDIENTS

FOR THE MARINADE

1 LEMONGRASS STALK, TENDER PART ONLY (THE BOTTOM HALF)

2 GARLIC CLOVES

1 TABLESPOON MINCED GINGER

1 SCALLION

¼ CUP BROWN SUGAR

2 TABLESPOONS CHILI PASTE

1 TABLESPOON SESAME OIL

1 TABLESPOON RICE VINEGAR

2 TABLESPOONS FISH SAUCE

1 TABLESPOON BLACK PEPPER

FOR THE CHICKEN THIGHS & VERMICELLI

10 OZ. SWEET POTATO VERMICELLI

2 TABLESPOONS VEGETABLE OIL

4-6 CHICKEN THIGHS

¼ HEAD OF NAPA CABBAGE, CHOPPED

4 OZ. SHIITAKE MUSHROOMS, SLICED THIN

1 SHALLOT, SLICED THIN

1 YELLOW ONION, SLICED THIN

2 GARLIC CLOVES, MINCED

Continued...

This is a Korean take on lo mein, the Chinese classic. The umami flavor of the sweet potato noodles, shiitake mushrooms, and cabbage is the perfect complement to the sweetness of the marinated chicken.

DIRECTIONS

1. To prepare the marinade, place all of the ingredients in a blender and blend until smooth. Pour over the chicken thighs and let them marinate in the refrigerator for at least 2 hours.

2. Fill a large cast-iron Dutch oven with water and bring to a boil. Add the vermicelli and cook for about 6 minutes. Drain, rinse with cold water to keep them from sticking, and set aside.

3. Preheat the oven to 375°F. Remove the chicken from the refrigerator and place the pot back on the stove. Add the vegetable oil and warm over medium-high heat. Remove the chicken thighs from the marinade and place them skin side down in the Dutch oven. Reserve the marinade. Sear the chicken until a crust forms on the skin, about 5 to 7 minutes. Turn the chicken thighs over, add the reserved marinade, place the pot in the oven, and cook for about 15 to 20 minutes, until the centers of the chicken thighs reach 165°F.

4. Remove from the oven and set the chicken aside. Drain the Dutch oven and wipe it clean. Return it to the stove, add the cabbage, mushrooms, shallot, onion, garlic, scallion whites, and ginger, and cook for 8 minutes or until the cabbage is wilted.

Continued...

2 SCALLIONS, CHOPPED,
GREENS RESERVED

2 TABLESPOONS MINCED GINGER

¼ CUP BROWN SUGAR

2 TABLESPOONS SESAME OIL

2 TABLESPOONS FISH SAUCE

¼ CUP SOY SAUCE

¼ CUP RICE VINEGAR

¼ CUP SESAME SEEDS

5. Add the brown sugar, sesame oil, fish sauce, soy sauce, and rice vinegar to a small bowl and stir until combined. Add this sauce and the vermicelli to the pot, stir until the noodles are coated, and then return the chicken thighs to the Dutch oven. Top with the scallion greens and sesame seeds, return to the oven for 5 minutes, and serve.

Duck Curry

YIELD: **4 SERVINGS**

ACTIVE TIME: **15 MINUTES**

TOTAL TIME: **30 MINUTES**

Your local store will likely have precooked duck breasts available for purchase, but it's worth cooking your own just to have access to the rich rendered fat that results from searing in cast iron.

INGREDIENTS

4 BONELESS, SKIN-ON DUCK BREASTS

¼ CUP THAI RED CURRY PASTE

2½ CUPS COCONUT MILK

10 MAKRUT LIME LEAVES (OPTIONAL)

1 CUP DICED PINEAPPLE

1 TABLESPOON FISH SAUCE, PLUS MORE TO TASTE

1 TABLESPOON BROWN SUGAR

6 BIRD'S EYE CHILIES, STEMMED

20 CHERRY TOMATOES

1 CUP BASIL (THAI BASIL STRONGLY PREFERRED)

1½ CUPS COOKED JASMINE RICE, FOR SERVING

DIRECTIONS

1. Use a very sharp knife to slash the skin on the duck breasts, while taking care not to cut all the way through to the meat.

2. Place a large cast-iron Dutch oven over medium-high heat. Place the duck breasts, skin side down, in the pot and sear until browned, about 4 minutes. This will render a lot of the fat.

3. Turn the duck breasts over and cook until browned on the other side, about 4 minutes. Remove the duck from the pot, let cool, and drain the rendered duck fat. Reserve the duck fat for another use.

4. When the duck breasts are cool enough to handle, remove the skin and discard. Cut each breast into 2-inch pieces.

5. Reduce the heat to medium, add the curry paste, and fry for 2 minutes. Add the coconut milk, bring to a boil, and cook for 5 minutes.

6. Reduce the heat, return the duck to the pot, and simmer for 8 minutes. Add the lime leaves, if using, the pineapple, fish sauce, brown sugar, and chilies, stir to incorporate, and simmer for 5 minutes. Skim to remove any fat from the top as the curry simmers.

7. Taste and add more fish sauce if needed. Stir in the cherry tomatoes and basil and serve alongside the rice.

Thai Basil Chicken

YIELD: **4 SERVINGS**

ACTIVE TIME: **10 MINUTES**

TOTAL TIME: **20 MINUTES**

The key to making this dish is finding Thai holy basil, which has a light anise flavor that is able to hold up to the heat—meaning both temperature and spice. If you can't find Thai holy basil, you can substitute any other kind and the dish will be nice, but not quite the same.

INGREDIENTS

¼ CUP FISH SAUCE

¼ CUP SOY SAUCE

¼ CUP WATER

2 TABLESPOONS BROWN SUGAR

4 BONELESS, SKINLESS CHICKEN BREASTS, CHOPPED

2 TABLESPOONS VEGETABLE OIL

2 SHALLOTS, SLICED THIN

2 RED BELL PEPPERS, SEEDED AND SLICED

2 FRESH RED BIRD'S EYE CHILIES, SLICED THIN

3 GARLIC CLOVES, ROUGHLY CHOPPED

1½ CUPS THAI BASIL LEAVES

DIRECTIONS

1. Place the fish sauce, soy sauce, water, and sugar in a bowl and stir to combine. Set half of the mixture aside, add the chicken, and let the chicken marinate for 10 minutes.

2. Place the oil in a large cast-iron wok or skillet and warm over medium-high heat. When the oil starts to shimmer, add the shallots, bell peppers, chilies, and garlic and sauté for 2 minutes, until the onion and garlic start to brown.

3. Use a slotted spoon to remove the chicken from the marinade and add the chicken to the hot pan. Cook, while stirring, until it is almost cooked through, about 3 minutes.

4. Add the reserved mixture and cook for another minute.

5. Remove the pan from heat and stir in 1 cup of the basil. Serve immediately, and top with the remaining Thai basil leaves.

Mojo Chicken

YIELD: **4 SERVINGS**

ACTIVE TIME: **30 MINUTES**

TOTAL TIME: **2½ TO 8½ HOURS**

This fiery, Cuban-inspired dish will wake up your taste buds every time. Ideally, it's made with sour orange juice—which is available at most Latin markets—but a combination of sweet orange and lemon juice works, too.

INGREDIENTS

1 YELLOW ONION, CHOPPED

10 GARLIC CLOVES, PEELED AND TRIMMED

2 SCOTCH BONNET PEPPERS, SEEDED AND CHOPPED

1 CUP CHOPPED CILANTRO LEAVES

1 TEASPOON DRIED THYME

1 TABLESPOON CUMIN

½ TEASPOON ALLSPICE

1 CUP ORANGE JUICE

½ CUP FRESH LEMON JUICE

½ TEASPOON CITRIC ACID (OPTIONAL)

ZEST AND JUICE OF 1 LIME

¼ CUP OLIVE OIL

4 BONELESS, SKINLESS CHICKEN BREASTS

SALT AND PEPPER, TO TASTE

DIRECTIONS

1. Place the onion, garlic, chilies, cilantro, thyme, cumin, allspice, orange juice, lemon juice, citric acid (if using), lime zest, lime juice, and olive oil in a food processor or blender and puree until smooth.

2. Pour the marinade into a resealable plastic bag and add the chicken. Let marinate for at least 2 hours and up to 8 hours, if time allows.

3. Preheat the oven to 350°F. Place a cast-iron grill pan over very high heat and warm.

4. Remove the chicken from the marinade and pat dry. Pour the marinade into a saucepan, bring to a boil over medium heat, and allow it to reduce as you cook the chicken.

5. When the pan is hot, add the chicken and cook until both sides are charred and the breasts are cooked through, about 4 minutes per side. The pan will start to smoke, so make sure an overhead fan is on or a window is open.

6. Season the sauce with salt and pepper and spoon it over the cooked chicken breasts.

CHAPTER 6

SEAFOOD

Bursting with freshness, delectable brininess, and subtle
sweetness, the bounties of oceans and fresh waters are ideal for
the quick cooking and ample heat supplied by cast iron. It is the only
material that can properly blacken tilapia (see page 167), and its
ability to crisp the skin of salmon (see pages 161 and 162)
adds another layer of loveliness to that rich fish.

Crab Cakes

YIELD: **6 CAKES**

ACTIVE TIME: **1 HOUR**

TOTAL TIME: **1 HOUR AND 30 MINUTES**

With these cakes, if you want great flavor, you have to go for top-quality crabmeat. This is the kind that's in the refrigerated section of your store's fish department. Don't buy crabmeat that's canned like tuna. It has neither the flavor nor the consistency needed for these cakes.

INGREDIENTS

FOR THE REMOULADE SAUCE

1 CUP MAYONNAISE

2 TABLESPOONS MUSTARD (CREOLE PREFERRED, OTHERWISE WHOLE GRAIN OR DIJON WILL DO)

1 TEASPOON CAJUN SEASONING

1 TABLESPOON SWEET PAPRIKA

1 TABLESPOON PICKLE JUICE OR FRESH LEMON JUICE

1 TABLESPOON LOUISIANA-STYLE HOT SAUCE, OR TO TASTE

1 GARLIC CLOVE, MINCED

2 TABLESPOONS MINCED FRESH PARSLEY (OPTIONAL)

SALT AND FRESHLY GROUND BLACK PEPPER, TO TASTE

FOR THE CRAB CAKES

1 LB. LUMP CRABMEAT (BLUE CRAB PREFERRED)

¼ CUP MINCED ONION

Continued...

DIRECTIONS

1. To prepare the sauce, place all of the ingredients in a bowl and stir to combine. Cover and chill in the refrigerator.

2. To prepare the crab cakes, in a large bowl, combine the crabmeat, onion, bread crumbs, Worcestershire sauce, Old Bay seasoning, hot sauce, parsley, and mayonnaise. Mix the milk into the egg and add to the crab mix, blending gently but thoroughly. Season with salt and pepper. If the mixture seems dry, add more mayonnaise.

3. Place a 12-inch cast-iron skillet over medium-high heat. Add the oil. It should be about ¼-inch deep. When oil is hot, add 3 or 4 individual heaping spoonfuls of crab mix to the skillet, pressing down on the tops of each to form a patty. Brown the cakes on each side for about 3 minutes. Try to turn the cakes over just once. If you're worried about them not getting cooked through, put a lid on the skillet for a minute or so after they've browned on each side.

4. Transfer the cakes to a plate and cover with foil to keep them warm while you cook the next batch.

5. Serve on a platter with lemon wedges and remoulade sauce on the side.

½ CUP BREAD CRUMBS

1 TEASPOON WORCESTERSHIRE
SAUCE

1 TEASPOON OLD BAY SEASONING

2 TABLESPOONS HOT SAUCE

1 TEASPOON DRIED PARSLEY

1 TABLESPOON MAYONNAISE

1 TABLESPOON WHOLE MILK

1 LARGE EGG, LIGHTLY BEATEN

SALT AND FRESHLY GROUND
PEPPER, TO TASTE

¼ CUP PEANUT OR OLIVE OIL

LEMON WEDGES, FOR SERVING

Seared Salmon

YIELD: **4 TO 6 SERVINGS**

ACTIVE TIME: **20 MINUTES**

TOTAL TIME: **30 MINUTES**

Start with super-fresh fish and keep it simple—butter, lemon, salt, and pepper—and you can create a succulent dish that is ready in no time.

INGREDIENTS

3-4 LBS. SKIN-ON SALMON FILLETS

2 TABLESPOONS UNSALTED BUTTER, AT ROOM TEMPERATURE AND CUT INTO PIECES

1 LEMON, HALVED

SALT AND PEPPER, TO TASTE

1 TABLESPOON OLIVE OIL

DIRECTIONS

1. Rinse the fillets with cold water to ensure that any scales or bones are removed and pat them dry with paper towels. Rub the butter on both sides of the fillets, squeeze lemon over them, and season with salt and pepper.

2. Place a 12-inch cast-iron skillet over medium-high heat and add the tablespoon of olive oil. Add the fillets, flesh side down. Cook on one side for about 3 minutes, then flip them and cook for 2 minutes on the other side. Remove the pan from heat and let the fish rest in it for a minute before serving. The skin should peel right off.

Honey-Glazed Salmon

YIELD: **4 SERVINGS**

ACTIVE TIME: **5 MINUTES**

TOTAL TIME: **15 MINUTES**

The rare recipe that is accessible for a beginner and still beloved by the most advanced chefs. The technique is straightforward and easy to master, and the results are nothing short of sublime. That it comes together in mere minutes is just another factor in its favor.

INGREDIENTS

4 SKIN-ON SALMON FILLETS

1 TABLESPOON OLIVE OIL

2 TABLESPOONS VEGETABLE OIL

KOSHER SALT, TO TASTE

3 TABLESPOONS HONEY

ZEST AND JUICE OF 1 LARGE LEMON

DIRECTIONS

1. Pat the salmon fillets dry with a paper towel. Rub the olive oil into them and season with salt.

2. Place a 12-inch cast-iron skillet over medium-high heat and add the vegetable oil. When it starts to shimmer, place the salmon fillets, skin side down, in the pan and cook for 8 minutes.

3. Reduce the heat to medium and use a spatula to carefully flip the salmon fillets over. Cook for another 8 minutes.

4. While the salmon is cooking, place the honey, lemon zest, and lemon juice in a bowl and stir to combine.

5. When the salmon is cooked through, remove from the skillet, drizzle the honey glaze over the top, and serve.

Teriyaki Salmon with Vegetables

YIELD: **4 SERVINGS**

ACTIVE TIME: **20 MINUTES**

TOTAL TIME: **20 MINUTES**

INGREDIENTS

FOR THE TERIYAKI SAUCE

1 TABLESPOON MINCED GINGER

2-3 GARLIC CLOVES, MINCED

1 TABLESPOON RICE OR WHITE VINEGAR

2 TABLESPOONS LIGHT BROWN SUGAR

¼ CUP LIGHT SOY SAUCE

1 TABLESPOON TAPIOCA STARCH OR CORNSTARCH

½ CUP WATER

FOR THE SALMON, CHINESE EGGPLANTS & BEAN SPROUTS

3 TABLESPOONS VEGETABLE OIL

4 CHINESE EGGPLANTS, CUT INTO ½-INCH-THICK SLICES ON A BIAS

1 RED BELL PEPPER, SEEDED AND JULIENNED

2 TABLESPOONS SCALLIONS, CHOPPED, GREENS RESERVED FOR GARNISH

1 CUP BEAN SPROUTS

1½ LBS. SKINLESS SALMON FILLETS

SALT AND PEPPER, TO TASTE

This recipe is perfect for people who are on the fence about seafood. Salmon is mild enough that it doesn't have an overpoweringly fishy taste and goes well with so many different preparations that it's a great way to ease a seafood nonbeliever into seeing the light. Plus, who can turn down homemade teriyaki sauce?

DIRECTIONS

1. To prepare the teriyaki sauce, place all of the ingredients in a blender and puree until smooth. Transfer to a small saucepan and cook, while stirring, until the sauce starts to thicken. Remove from heat and set aside.

2. Preheat your oven to 375°F. Place the oil in a 12-inch cast-iron skillet and warm over medium-high heat. Add the eggplants, bell pepper, and scallion whites to the pan and cook for 5 minutes, while stirring occasionally. Add the bean sprouts and stir until all the vegetables are evenly coated by the oil.

3. Place your salmon on the vegetables, flesh side up. Season with salt, pepper, and teriyaki sauce and transfer the pan to the oven. Cook for 8 to 10 minutes, remove the pan from the oven, top with more teriyaki sauce, and serve.

Sweet and Smoky Salmon

YIELD: **4 SERVINGS**

ACTIVE TIME: **10 MINUTES**

TOTAL TIME: **1 HOUR**

Smoking food brings a whole different dimension of flavor that's totally worth exploring. A brief kiss can add a woodsy umami flavor, while a good long time in the smoker brings something wild and unctuous to the table.

INGREDIENTS

½ CUP VEGETABLE OIL, PLUS MORE AS NEEDED

½ CUP MIRIN

1 TABLESPOON BROWN SUGAR

1 TABLESPOON MINCED GINGER

1 TEASPOON ORANGE ZEST

1 LB. SKINLESS, CENTER-CUT SALMON FILLETS

1 CUP WHITE RICE

½ CUP GRANULATED SUGAR

1 CUP GREEN TEA (GUNPOWDER PREFERRED)

1 ORANGE PEEL, DICED

DIRECTIONS

1. In a shallow dish, whisk together the oil, mirin, brown sugar, ginger, and orange zest. Add the salmon and let marinate for 30 minutes.

2. Line a large cast-iron wok with foil. You want the foil to extend over the sides of the wok. Add the rice, granulated sugar, tea, and orange peel and cook over high heat until the rice begins to smoke.

3. Place the salmon on a lightly oiled rack, set it above the smoking rice, and place the lid on top of wok. Fold the foil over the lid to seal the wok as best as you can.

4. Reduce heat to medium and cook for 10 minutes.

5. Remove from heat and let the wok cool completely, about 20 minutes. When done, the fish will be cooked to medium. Serve immediately.

Cajun Tilapia

YIELD: **4 SERVINGS**

ACTIVE TIME: **40 MINUTES**

TOTAL TIME: **1 HOUR AND 30 MINUTES**

The cast-iron skillet is perfect for blackening fish, which requires high heat and quick cooking. Tilapia is wonderful for blackening, as it is a firm-fleshed fish that is fairly bland and thus benefits from generous seasoning. Although the result is delicious, the blackening process creates a lot of smoke, so be sure to turn on the oven fan or open the windows before you start cooking.

INGREDIENTS

2 TABLESPOONS PAPRIKA

1 TABLESPOON ONION POWDER

3 TABLESPOONS GARLIC POWDER

2 TABLESPOONS CAYENNE PEPPER

1½ TEASPOONS CELERY SALT

1½ TABLESPOONS BLACK PEPPER

1 TABLESPOON DRIED THYME

1 TABLESPOON DRIED OREGANO

1 TABLESPOON CHIPOTLE POWDER

4 (4 OZ.) BONELESS
TILAPIA FILLETS

1 STICK OF UNSALTED
BUTTER, MELTED

1 LEMON, CUT INTO 4 WEDGES,
FOR SERVING

DIRECTIONS

1. In a bowl, combine all the spices and set aside.

2. Place a 12-inch cast-iron skillet over high heat for about 10 minutes until very hot. While the skillet heats up, rinse the fillets and then pat dry with paper towels. Dip the fillets in the melted butter, covering both sides, and then press the seasoning mixture generously into both sides.

3. Put the fish in the skillet and cook for about 3 minutes per side, placing a bit of butter on top while the other side is cooking. Serve with lemon wedges.

Halibut Over Coconut Milk Vegetables

YIELD: **4 TO 6 SERVINGS**

ACTIVE TIME: **30 MINUTES**

TOTAL TIME: **1 HOUR**

INGREDIENTS

¼ CUP OLIVE OIL

1 YELLOW BELL PEPPER, DICED

1 RED BELL PEPPER, DICED

1 HABANERO PEPPER, PIERCED

1 LARGE OR 2 SMALL WHITE SWEET POTATOES

1 CUP DICED RED CABBAGE

SALT AND PEPPER, TO TASTE

3 GRAFFITI EGGPLANT, CUT INTO 2-INCH PIECES

2 TABLESPOONS MASHED GINGER

3-4 GARLIC CLOVES, MINCED

1-2 TABLESPOONS GREEN CURRY PASTE

2-3 BABY BOK CHOY, CHOPPED

4 CUPS FISH STOCK

1-2 TABLESPOONS SWEET PAPRIKA

2 TABLESPOONS CHOPPED CILANTRO

3 (14 OZ.) CANS OF UNSWEETENED COCONUT MILK

LEAVES FROM 2 BUNCHES OF TUSCAN KALE, TORN INTO LARGE PIECES

4-6 (4 OZ.) HALIBUT FILLETS

SCALLIONS, CHOPPED, FOR GARNISH

The kale is key to this one, providing a nice, soft bed for the halibut and ensuring that it remains moist and full of flavor.

DIRECTIONS

1. Place the oil in a cast-iron Dutch oven and warm over medium-high heat. Add the bell peppers, habanero, sweet potatoes, and cabbage. Season with salt and pepper and cook, while stirring, for 5 to 7 minutes or until the sweet potatoes begin to caramelize.

2. Add the eggplant, ginger, and garlic and cook, while stirring often, for 10 minutes. Add the curry paste and stir to coat all of the vegetables. Cook for 2 minutes or until the contents of the pot are fragrant.

3. Add the bok choy, stock, paprika, cilantro, and coconut milk and cook for 15 to 25 minutes, until the liquid has been reduced by one-quarter.

4. Add the kale to the Dutch oven. Place the halibut fillets on top of the kale, reduce the heat to medium, cover, and cook for about 10 minutes or until the fish is cooked through.

5. Remove the cover and discard the habanero. Ladle the vegetables and the sauce into the bowls and top each one with a halibut fillet. Garnish with the scallions and serve.

Tomatillo Sauce Simmered Red Snapper

YIELD: **4 SERVINGS**

ACTIVE TIME: **10 MINUTES**

TOTAL TIME: **10 MINUTES**

This recipe comes together in under 15 minutes, but it's still as joyous and awe-inspiring as a fireworks show on the Fourth of July thanks to the charred vegetables.

INGREDIENTS

1 LB. TOMATILLOS, HUSKED, RINSED, AND QUARTERED

½ WHITE ONION, CHOPPED

1 GARLIC CLOVE, CRUSHED

1 SERRANO PEPPER, STEMMED (OPTIONAL)

1 BUNCH OF FRESH CILANTRO, SOME LEAVES RESERVED FOR GARNISH

2 TABLESPOONS CORN OR VEGETABLE OIL

1½ LBS. SKINLESS RED SNAPPER FILLETS

LIME WEDGES, FOR SERVING

GRILLED VEGETABLES, FOR SERVING

DIRECTIONS

1. Place a dry 12-inch cast-iron skillet over high heat and add the tomatillos, onion, garlic, and serrano pepper (if using). Cook until charred slightly and then transfer them to a blender. Add the bunch of cilantro and puree until smooth.

2. Place the oil in a 12-inch cast-iron skillet and warm over medium-high heat. When the oil starts to shimmer, add the red snapper fillets in a single layer, skin side down, and cook until they brown lightly. Do not turn them over.

3. Remove the pan from heat and allow it to cool for a few minutes. Carefully pour the tomatillo sauce over the fish. It will immediately start to simmer.

4. Place the skillet over medium heat and let it simmer until the fish is cooked through, about 4 minutes.

5. Garnish with the reserved cilantro and serve with the lime wedges and grilled vegetables.

New England-Style Fish & Chips

YIELD: **2 TO 4 SERVINGS**

ACTIVE TIME: **20 MINUTES**

TOTAL TIME: **45 MINUTES**

This New England twist on a British favorite is a must-try dish. Cook this up at the height of pollock season to really capture the essence of the fresh fish paired with the delicious cornmeal breading.

INGREDIENTS

4 CUPS CANOLA OIL

5 POTATOES, SLICED INTO LONG, THIN STRIPS

3 TABLESPOONS MINCED FRESH ROSEMARY LEAVES

SALT AND PEPPER, TO TASTE

2 EGGS, BEATEN

1 CUP CORNMEAL

1-1½ LBS. POLLOCK FILLETS

DIRECTIONS

1. Place the canola oil in a cast-iron Dutch oven and bring to 350°F over medium-high heat.

2. When the oil is ready, place the sliced potatoes in the oil and cook until golden brown. Remove and set to drain on a paper towel–lined plate. Keep the oil at 350°F.

3. When drained to your liking, place the fried potatoes in a bowl with the rosemary and salt and toss to coat. Set aside.

4. Place the beaten eggs in a small bowl and the cornmeal in another. Dip the pollock fillets into the egg and then into the cornmeal, repeating until coated all over.

5. Place the battered pollock in the oil and cook until golden brown. Remove and set to drain on another paper towel–lined plate. Serve with the rosemary chips.

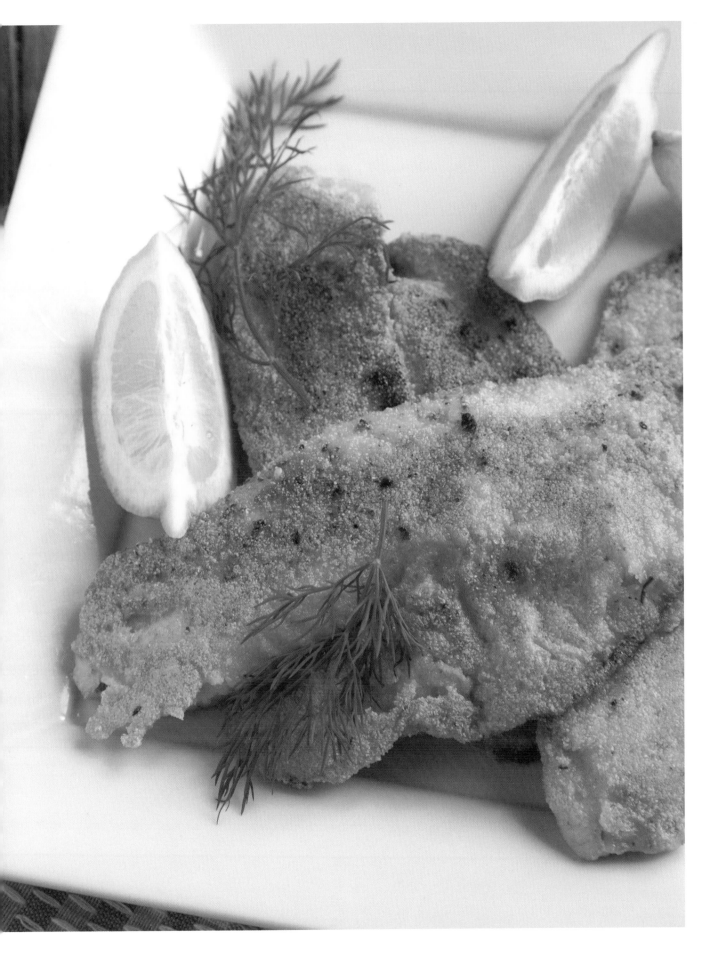

Pasta and Littleneck Clams

YIELD: **4 TO 6 SERVINGS**

ACTIVE TIME: **15 TO 20 MINUTES**

TOTAL TIME: **30 TO 40 MINUTES**

Easy, salty, and bursting with freshness. If you don't have much time but need to whip up something special, this dish won't let you down.

INGREDIENTS

1 LB. LINGUINE

2 TABLESPOONS SEA SALT

½ CUP OLIVE OIL

3 GARLIC CLOVES, SLICED THIN

32 LITTLENECK CLAMS, SCRUBBED AND RINSED

1 CUP WHITE WINE

1 CUP CLAM JUICE

1 CUP CHOPPED ITALIAN PARSLEY

¼ CUP GRATED PARMESAN CHEESE

SALT AND PEPPER, TO TASTE

DIRECTIONS

1. In a cast-iron Dutch oven, bring 4 quarts of water to a boil. Add the linguine and the sea salt. Cook for 7 minutes or until the pasta is just short of al dente. Drain, while reserving ½ cup of cooking water, and then set the linguine aside.

2. Place the Dutch oven over medium heat. Add half of the olive oil and all of the garlic to the pot and cook until the garlic starts to brown, about 2 minutes. Add the clams and wine, cover, and cook for 5 to 7 minutes or until the majority of the clams are open. Use a slotted spoon to transfer the clams to a colander. Discard any clams that do not open.

3. Add the clam juice, parsley, and pasta water to the Dutch oven. Cook until the sauce starts to thicken, about 10 minutes. Remove all the clams from their shells and mince one-quarter of them.

4. Return the linguine to the pot. Add the Parmesan, season with salt and pepper, and stir until the cheese begins to melt. Fold in the clams, drizzle with the remaining olive oil, and serve.

TIP: If you do not have access to fresh clams, you can use canned whole clams.

Basque-Style Clams

YIELD: **4 TO 6 SERVINGS**

ACTIVE TIME: **15 MINUTES**

TOTAL TIME: **15 MINUTES**

Hailing from Spain's Basque population, this heady dish is as unique as the people who inhabit the region. Flavorful and light, it is perfect as part of a tapas-style meal.

INGREDIENTS

24 LITTLENECK CLAMS, SCRUBBED AND RINSED

1 TABLESPOON OLIVE OIL

1 YELLOW ONION, CHOPPED

3 GARLIC CLOVES, MINCED

2 CUPS CHERRY TOMATOES

2 OZ. SPANISH CHORIZO, MINCED

2 TABLESPOONS UNSALTED BUTTER, CUT INTO SMALL PIECES

DIRECTIONS

1. Pick over the clams and discard any that are open, cracked, or damaged.

2. Place the olive oil in a 12-inch cast-iron skillet and warm over medium heat. When the oil starts to shimmer, add the onion and cook, without stirring, for 2 minutes. Add the garlic and tomatoes and cook, while stirring occasionally, until the tomatoes are browned and just beginning to burst, about 5 minutes. Add the chorizo, stir to incorporate, and cook for another 2 minutes.

3. Add the clams, cover the pot, and let them steam until the majority of the clams have opened, about 2 minutes.

4. Remove any clams that haven't opened and discard. Add the butter and stir until the butter has melted. Serve warm or at room temperature.

Baked Mussels & Orzo

YIELD: **4 TO 6 SERVINGS**

ACTIVE TIME: **30 MINUTES**

TOTAL TIME: **45 MINUTES**

The subtle sweetness of Prince Edward Island mussels lends this dish tons of flavor, and the mussels are perfectly sized when you take the rest of the dish's components into account. There's a lot of juice to sop up in this one, so serve with a warm loaf of bread and plenty of napkins.

INGREDIENTS

3 LBS. P.E.I. MUSSELS

3 TABLESPOONS OLIVE OIL, PLUS MORE AS NEEDED

2 GARLIC CLOVES, SLICED THIN

1 LARGE SHALLOT, SLICED THIN

4 SCALLIONS, SLICED THIN, GREENS RESERVED FOR GARNISH

1 CUP ORZO

¼ CUP SUN-DRIED TOMATOES, SLICED THIN

2 PINTS OF CHERRY TOMATOES

1½ CUPS CHICKEN STOCK (SEE PAGE 137)

½ CUP WHITE WINE

2 TABLESPOONS UNSALTED BUTTER

SALT AND PEPPER, TO TASTE

½ CUP CHOPPED BASIL LEAVES, FOR GARNISH

1 LOAF OF CRUSTY BREAD, WARMED AND SLICED

DIRECTIONS

1. Sort through the mussels and remove any open, cracked, or damaged ones. Next, use a thin kitchen towel and remove the "beards," which are the brown threads extending from where the two shells meet. Pull the threads toward the hinge until the beard separates from the mussel. Not every mussel will have a beard, so don't panic if you don't find one.

2. Preheat the oven to 350°F. Heat a 12-inch cast-iron skillet over medium-high heat and add the oil. When the oil is warm, add the garlic, shallot, and scallion whites and sauté for 3 minutes, while stirring constantly. Add the orzo and sun-dried tomatoes and stir to coat. Cook, while stirring occasionally, for about 10 minutes, until the orzo is slightly toasted.

3. Add the cherry tomatoes, stock, and white wine and transfer the skillet to the oven. Cook for about 10 minutes, until the orzo is cooked through and the tomatoes begin to split open.

4. Remove the skillet from the oven and place the hinge of each mussel into the orzo. Make sure the openings of the mussels are facing upward. Return to the oven and cook for 5 to 7 minutes, until the majority of the mussels are open. Remove from the oven and discard any unopened mussels. Drizzle with olive oil, season to taste, garnish with the basil and scallion greens, and serve with warm bread.

TIP: When you bring the mussels home from the market, put them in a bowl of fresh water with a ¼ of all-purpose flour until you begin to prepare the ingredients for the rest of the dish.

Coconut Milk Mussels

YIELD: **4 SERVINGS**

ACTIVE TIME: **15 MINUTES**

TOTAL TIME: **25 MINUTES**

The combination of sweet, sour, and spicy that Thai cuisine is famous for is on full display in this delightful and flavorful dish. Tinker with the amount of lime juice until you get it just right, and don't be afraid to squeeze a little bit of lemon juice in there instead.

INGREDIENTS

2 LBS. MUSSELS

½ CUP CILANTRO LEAVES AND STEMS

1 TABLESPOON VEGETABLE OIL

4 SHALLOTS, MINCED

2 GARLIC CLOVES, SLICED

1 LEMONGRASS STALK, CUT INTO 4 LARGE PIECES

1 BIRD'S EYE CHILI PEPPER, STEMMED AND SLICED

1 (14 OZ.) CAN OF COCONUT MILK

1 TABLESPOON FISH SAUCE (OPTIONAL)

JUICE OF 1 LIME

½ LB. COOKED RICE NOODLES, FOR SERVING (OPTIONAL)

1 LB. COOKED WHITE RICE, FOR SERVING (OPTIONAL)

DIRECTIONS

1. Wash the mussels thoroughly and discard any that aren't tightly closed.

2. Remove the cilantro leaves from the stems. Set the leaves aside and finely chop the stems.

3. Place the vegetable oil in a large cast-iron Dutch oven and warm until it is shimmering. Add the shallots, garlic, chopped cilantro stems, lemongrass, and the bird's eye chili and cook, while stirring, until the garlic is lightly browned, about 4 minutes.

4. Add the coconut milk and the fish sauce (if using) and bring to a boil. Add the mussels and immediately cover the pot.

5. Steam until the majority of the mussels are opened and the meat is still plump, about 5 minutes. Be careful not to overcook the mussels, as it will cause them to have a rubbery texture. Discard any unopened mussels.

6. Stir a few times to coat the mussels and add half of the lime juice. Taste and add more lime juice as needed. Ladle into warmed bowls, garnish with the reserved cilantro leaves, and serve with the rice noodles or white rice.

Buttery Garlic Shrimp

YIELD: **4 SERVINGS**

ACTIVE TIME: **5 MINUTES**

TOTAL TIME: **10 MINUTES**

What's not to like here? Sweet, briny shrimp, loads of luscious butter, and a bit of mellowed garlic, all held together by the acidic kick of lemon. A culinary wonder that shines when made in cast iron.

INGREDIENTS

4 TABLESPOONS UNSALTED BUTTER, AT ROOM TEMPERATURE

1 LB. SHRIMP, PEELED AND DEVEINED

8 GARLIC CLOVES, MINCED

½ TEASPOON LEMON-PEPPER SEASONING

2 TEASPOONS FRESH LEMON JUICE

1 TEASPOON MINCED CHIVES OR PARSLEY, FOR GARNISH

1 RED CHILI PEPPER, SLICED THIN, FOR GARNISH (OPTIONAL)

DIRECTIONS

1. Place a 10-inch cast-iron skillet over medium heat and add the butter.

2. When the butter has melted and is foaming, add the shrimp and cook, without stirring, for 2 minutes. Remove from the pan and set aside.

3. Reduce the heat to medium-low and add the garlic and lemon-pepper seasoning. Cook until the garlic has softened, about 2 minutes. Return the shrimp to the pan and cooked until warmed through, about 1 minute.

4. To serve, sprinkle with the lemon juice and garnish with the chives and chili pepper, if desired.

CHAPTER 7

VEGETABLES

———————————

There was a time, not too long ago, when people
shied away from a little char on their vegetables but gladly
boiled them into a sad, defeated state. By embracing fresh flavor
and learning how to enhance it with seasoning, we've come to show
respect for the produce our farmers work so hard to harvest. Using your
cast-iron cookware, you can create truly masterful vegetable dishes that
will appeal to vegetarians, vegans, and meat-eaters alike. Try a new-to-
you vegetable—perhaps the Creamed Greens (see page 197) piques
your interest—or go with one of the twists on an old classic,
such as Green Beans with Bacon, the ideal cast-
iron skillet recipe (see page 208).

Roasted Cauliflower Medallions

YIELD: **4 TO 6 SERVINGS**

ACTIVE TIME: **30 MINUTES**

TOTAL TIME: **1 HOUR**

There's something about roasting cauliflower that accentuates its sweet, nutty flavor. Season it with warm, earthy spices like cumin and turmeric, and you have a delicious alternative to a starchy side, full of flavor and nutrition.

INGREDIENTS

1½ TABLESPOONS OLIVE OIL

1 TEASPOON SALT

FRESHLY GROUND PEPPER, TO TASTE

½ TEASPOON CUMIN

½ TEASPOON CORIANDER

½ TEASPOON TURMERIC

¼ TEASPOON CAYENNE PEPPER

1 HEAD OF CAULIFLOWER, TRIMMED

SOUR CREAM, FOR SERVING (OPTIONAL)

DIRECTIONS

1. Preheat the oven to 425°F.

2. In a bowl, combine the oil, salt, pepper, and spices and whisk to mix thoroughly.

3. Cut the cauliflower cross-wise into ½-inch slices. Put the slices in the skillet and brush the tops liberally with the oil mixture. Turn the "steaks" over and brush the other side.

4. Put the steaks in a 12-inch cast-iron skillet, place the skillet in the oven, and roast for about 20 minutes, turning the pieces over after 10 minutes. A toothpick inserted in the flesh should go in easily to indicate that the cauliflower is cooked through.

5. Serve the slices hot, with a side of sour cream, if desired.

TIP: This recipe can be made with cauliflower florets, too. Instead of slicing the cauliflower into cross sections, just pick off the florets. Put them in the bowl of seasoned oil and toss to coat. Put the florets in the skillet and bake, shaking the pan halfway through to turn the pieces.

Pan-Fried Shishito Peppers

YIELD: **4 TO 6 SERVINGS**

ACTIVE TIME: **5 MINUTES**

TOTAL TIME: **10 MINUTES**

Shishito peppers are slightly twisted, bright green, and utterly delicious. Eating them is a bit like putting your taste buds through a round of Russian roulette, since approximately one in every ten is spicy, and there's no way to tell until you bite down. The rest are as mild as can be. If you can't find shishitos, you can easily substitute padrón peppers.

INGREDIENTS

OLIVE OIL, FOR FRYING

2 LBS. SHISHITO PEPPERS

MALDON SEA SALT, TO TASTE

1 LEMON, CUT INTO WEDGES, FOR SERVING

DIRECTIONS

1. Add olive oil to a 12-inch cast-iron skillet until it is ¼-inch deep and warm over medium heat.

2. When the oil is shimmering, add the peppers and cook, while turning once or twice, until they are blistered and golden brown, about 2 minutes. Take care not to crowd the peppers in the pan, and work in batches if necessary.

3. Transfer the blistered peppers to a paper towel–lined plate. Season with salt and serve with lemon wedges.

Cast-Iron Asparagus

YIELD: **4 SERVINGS**

ACTIVE TIME: **20 MINUTES**

TOTAL TIME: **30 MINUTES**

Making asparagus in the skillet is almost like cooking it on the grill. The outside gets crisp while the inside becomes tender. The thinner the asparagus, the faster the stalks will cook, so if you are working with super-fresh, thin stalks, you may need to reduce the cooking times in the recipe.

INGREDIENTS

3 TABLESPOONS OLIVE OIL

1 BUNCH OF THIN ASPARAGUS, WOODY ENDS REMOVED

1 GARLIC CLOVE, MINCED

½ TEASPOON SALT

½ TEASPOON FRESHLY GROUND PEPPER

LEMON WEDGES, FOR SERVING

DIRECTIONS

1. Place a 12-inch cast-iron skillet over medium-high heat. When hot, add the oil and let that get hot. Add the asparagus. Using tongs, keep turning them so they cook evenly in the oil. Cook the asparagus until they are bright green and hot on the outside but tender on the inside.

2. Add the garlic, salt, and pepper, and shake the pan to distribute evenly. Cook for another 2 minutes. Transfer to a serving platter and serve with lemon wedges.

Winter Vegetable Roast

YIELD: **4 TO 6 SERVINGS**

ACTIVE TIME: **20 MINUTES**

TOTAL TIME: **1 HOUR**

If you find yourself at home on a fall morning with bunches of root vegetables that looked so good at the farmers market but are now baffling you as a cook, this recipe is here to save the day.

INGREDIENTS

2 SMALL PARSNIPS, TRIMMED, SCRUBBED, AND CUT INTO BATONS

1 TURNIP, TRIMMED, SCRUBBED, AND CUT INTO BATONS

4 SMALL BEETS, TRIMMED, SCRUBBED, AND CUT INTO BATONS

4 CARROTS, TRIMMED, SCRUBBED, AND CUT INTO BATONS

½ ONION, SLICED

1 SMALL BULB FENNEL, TRIMMED AND CUT INTO MATCHSTICKS

¼ CUP OLIVE OIL

SALT AND PEPPER, TO TASTE

2 TEASPOONS DRIED ROSEMARY

DIRECTIONS

1. Preheat the oven to 400°F.

2. In a large bowl, combine all the vegetables and pour the olive oil over them. Season with salt and pepper and toss to coat.

3. Put the vegetables in a 12-inch cast-iron skillet and sprinkle the rosemary over everything.

4. Put the skillet in the oven and bake for about 40 minutes, turning the vegetables over after the first 20 minutes. Serve warm.

VARIATION: Substitute Herbes de Provence for the rosemary. This is a French blend of rosemary, fennel, basil, thyme, marjoram, basil, tarragon, and lavender—all the goodness of a Provençal herb garden.

Mushroom Medley

YIELD: **4 SERVINGS**

ACTIVE TIME: **20 MINUTES**

TOTAL TIME: **30 MINUTES**

There are many kinds of mushrooms available, and you can mix and match them as you desire. Sautéing mushrooms in the skillet with lots of butter yields a rich, earthy side that is delicious with steak and potatoes. Or simply use these mushrooms as a topping for burgers or baked polenta with cheese.

INGREDIENTS

6 TABLESPOONS UNSALTED BUTTER, CUT INTO SMALL PIECES

1 LB. MUSHROOMS, SLICED

1 TEASPOON DRY VERMOUTH

SALT AND PEPPER, TO TASTE

DIRECTIONS

1. Place a 12-inch cast-iron skillet over medium-high heat. Add the butter. When melted, add the mushrooms. Cook, while stirring, until the mushrooms begin to soften, about 5 minutes. Reduce the heat to low and let the mushrooms simmer, stirring occasionally, until they cook down, about 15 to 20 minutes.

2. Add the vermouth and stir, then season with salt and pepper. Simmer until the mushrooms are tender. Serve hot.

Creamed Pearl Onions

YIELD: **8 SERVINGS**

ACTIVE TIME: **35 MINUTES**

TOTAL TIME: **35 MINUTES**

A rich, comforting dish that is right at home beside a roasted chicken or turkey. Fresh pearl onions are ideal, but in the interest of saving time, frozen pearl onions will do. They come in red or white, and a mix of the two makes for a visually stunning presentation. If you're lucky to live in an area where shallots are abundant, don't hesitate to toss a few of those in, too.

INGREDIENTS

2½ TABLESPOONS UNSALTED BUTTER

2 TABLESPOONS ALL-PURPOSE FLOUR

1½ CUPS CHICKEN STOCK (SEE PAGE 137)

½ CUP HEAVY CREAM, AT ROOM TEMPERATURE

½ CUP DRY WHITE WINE

¼ TEASPOON GROUND DRIED SAGE

1 LB. FROZEN PEARL ONIONS, THAWED AND DRAINED

SALT AND PEPPER, TO TASTE

DIRECTIONS

1. Place 2 tablespoons of the butter in a 12-inch cast-iron skillet and melt over medium-low heat. Add the flour and cook, while stirring constantly, until it is golden brown, about 6 minutes. Gradually whisk in the stock and bring to a boil, whisking until the roux is smooth. Remove the skillet from heat and whisk in the cream.

2. Place the skillet over medium-high heat and cook, while stirring frequently, until the sauce thickens, about 8 minutes.

3. Add the wine and sage and cook, while stirring, until the sauce has further thickened, about 2 minutes.

4. Add the onions and reduce heat to medium. Cook, while stirring frequently, until all of the onions are warmed through, about 6 minutes.

5. Whisk in the remaining butter, season with salt and pepper, and serve immediately.

Creamed Greens

YIELD: **4 SERVINGS**

ACTIVE TIME: **5 MINUTES**

TOTAL TIME: **20 MINUTES**

This dish is a brassica lover's dream, and it will change the mind of anyone who doesn't love greens. The mustard powder pulls double duty here, adding a burst of flavor and helping to thicken the sauce. If you can find rainbow chard, use that: the pretty red-and-yellow stems will make the dish Insta-worthy.

INGREDIENTS

2 TABLESPOONS COCONUT OIL

4 CUPS SHREDDED KALE LEAVES

2 TEASPOONS MUSTARD POWDER

1 CUP HEAVY CREAM

¼ CUP WATER

1 LARGE BUNCH OF SWISS CHARD, LEAVES AND STEMS CHOPPED

SALT, TO TASTE

DIRECTIONS

1. Place the coconut oil in a large cast-iron Dutch oven and warm over medium-high heat.

2. When the oil is shimmering, add the kale and stir to coat. Cook until the greens are wilted, about 5 minutes.

3. Add the mustard powder, cream, and water. Stir to incorporate, reduce the heat to medium-low, cover, and simmer for 5 minutes.

4. Remove the lid and stir in the Swiss chard. Cover again and simmer until the chard is wilted, about 2 minutes. Season with salt and serve.

Roasted Radicchio

YIELD: **4 SERVINGS**

ACTIVE TIME: **10 MINUTES**

TOTAL TIME: **1 HOUR AND 30 MINUTES**

If you like tart and bitter vegetables, this dish is for you. Just make sure the skillet is screaming hot before you add the radicchio, since you want it to be charred before adding the rest of the marinade.

INGREDIENTS

¼ CUP OLIVE OIL

8 GARLIC CLOVES, MINCED

2 TEASPOONS MINCED ROSEMARY LEAVES

¼ CUP BALSAMIC VINEGAR

1 ANCHOVY FILLET, SMASHED (OPTIONAL)

SALT AND PEPPER, TO TASTE

4 HEADS OF RADICCHIO, HALVED THROUGH THE ROOT

PARMESAN CHEESE, GRATED, FOR GARNISH

DIRECTIONS

1. Preheat the oven to 425°F.

2. Place the olive oil, garlic, rosemary, vinegar, anchovy (if using), salt, and pepper in a large bowl and stir to combine. Add the radicchio to the bowl and carefully toss to coat. Let the radicchio marinate for 1 hour.

3. Place a 12-inch cast-iron skillet over high heat for 10 minutes, until it is extremely hot. Using tongs, remove the radicchio from the marinade and arrange, cut side down, in the skillet. Let it sear for a few minutes.

4. Reduce the heat and pour the marinade over the radicchio. Place the skillet in the oven and roast until the radicchio is tender, about 20 minutes. Remove and garnish with the Parmesan before serving.

Sauted Spinach

YIELD: **6 TO 8 SERVINGS**

ACTIVE TIME: **10 MINUTES**

TOTAL TIME: **10 MINUTES**

Using mellow-flavored shallots instead of the usual garlic and onions keeps the spinach flavor bright in this quick-cooking dish. A splash of balsamic vinegar takes it over the top.

INGREDIENTS

3 TABLESPOONS OLIVE OIL

4 LARGE SHALLOTS, SLICED THIN

2 LBS. FRESH SPINACH, STEMMED, RINSED, AND THOROUGHLY DRIED

1 TABLESPOON BALSAMIC VINEGAR

SALT AND PEPPER, TO TASTE

DIRECTIONS

1. Place a 12-inch cast-iron skillet over medium-high heat. Add the olive oil and shallots and cook, while stirring, until shallots are translucent, about 2 minutes.

2. Add the spinach and cook, while stirring, until the leaves are covered by the oil and shallots, about 2 or 3 minutes. The spinach will start to wilt quickly. Reduce the heat and keep stirring so none of it burns. If desired, you can turn the heat to low and cover the skillet so the spinach steams.

3. When the spinach leaves are wilted and still bright green, splash them with the balsamic vinegar, shaking the pan to distribute. Season with salt and pepper and serve.

TIP: This dish works best with more mature spinach. Reserve baby spinach greens for salads and use the larger leaves for this dish.

Stuffed Tomatoes

YIELD: **6 SERVINGS**

ACTIVE TIME: **1 HOUR**

TOTAL TIME: **2 HOURS**

If you want to make this without sausage, simply omit it, double the quantity of mushrooms, and, after sautéing the mushrooms and peppers, drain the excess liquid. You can also add toasted walnut pieces for additional flavor and fiber.

INGREDIENTS

6 LARGE RIPE TOMATOES

SALT AND PEPPER, TO TASTE

1 LB. SAUSAGE, CASINGS REMOVED

1 ONION, DICED

4 GARLIC CLOVES, MINCED

8 WHITE MUSHROOMS, STEMMED AND DICED

½ GREEN BELL PEPPER, SEEDED AND DICED

2 TEASPOONS RED PEPPER FLAKES (OPTIONAL)

2 CUPS BREAD CRUMBS

2 TABLESPOONS DRIED SAGE

1 CUP GRATED PARMESAN CHEESE

OLIVE OIL, AS NEEDED

DIRECTIONS

1. Preheat the oven to 375°F.

2. Cut off the tops of the tomatoes, and use a small paring knife or a serrated grapefruit spoon to scoop out the insides. Once hollowed, sprinkle salt on the insides and turn upside down on a plate covered with a paper towel to absorb the water. Let sit for about 30 minutes.

3. Heat a 12-inch cast-iron skillet over medium-high heat and cook the sausage, breaking it up with a wooden spoon as it cooks. Cook until there is no pink showing in the meat. When cooked, use a slotted spoon to transfer the sausage to a large bowl. In the sausage fat, cook the onion and garlic until the onion is translucent, about 4 minutes. Add the mushrooms and bell pepper and cook over medium heat, while stirring, until vegetables soften, about 10 minutes. Add red pepper flakes, if desired.

4. Add the mushroom mixture to the sausage and stir to combine. Then add the bread crumbs, sage, and Parmesan. Season with salt and pepper.

5. Wipe down the skillet and brush with olive oil. Position the tomatoes in the skillet, bottoms down. Start filling the tomatoes gently, dividing the filling between them. Cover the skillet with aluminum foil and put the skillet in the oven. Bake for about 30 minutes, remove the foil, and continue baking for another 10 to 15 minutes, until cooked through. Serve hot.

Fried Artichokes with Gremolata

YIELD: **2 TO 4 SERVINGS**

ACTIVE TIME: **20 MINUTES**

TOTAL TIME: **30 MINUTES**

This beautiful dish is one of the classics in Roman Jewish cuisine, where it is known as **carciofi alla giudia.** *Like so many culinary cornerstones, it's simple: fry tender artichokes until crisp and dress with an Italian gremolata. The key is seasoning the artichokes with the correct amount of salt after they come out of the oil, so don't be afraid to experiment until you get it just right.*

INGREDIENTS

ZEST AND JUICE OF 2 LARGE LEMONS

2 CUPS WATER

½ CUP MINCED PARSLEY

7 GARLIC CLOVES, 6 MINCED, 1 WHOLE

3 LBS. BABY ARTICHOKES, TRIMMED

OLIVE OIL, FOR FRYING

SALT, TO TASTE

DIRECTIONS

1. Place the lemon zest in a small bowl. Place the lemon juice in a separate bowl. Add the water to the lemon juice, stir to combine, and set aside.

2. Add the parsley and the minced garlic to the lemon zest, stir to combine, and set the gremolata aside.

3. Cut any large artichokes in half lengthwise. Place all of the artichokes in the lemon water. Line a baking sheet with paper towels and place it near the stovetop.

4. Add olive oil to a cast-iron Dutch oven until it is ½ inch deep. Warm over medium heat for 4 minutes and then drop in the whole garlic clove. Remove the garlic when the oil starts to bubble.

5. Drain the artichokes and pat dry. Working in three batches, drop the artichokes into the oil and fry, while turning occasionally, until golden brown, about 5 minutes. Carefully remove the fried artichokes and transfer them to the lined baking sheet. Sprinkle with salt, garnish with the gremolata, and serve.

Sweet Corn Succotash

YIELD: **8 TO 10 SERVINGS**

ACTIVE TIME: **30 MINUTES**

TOTAL TIME: **1 HOUR**

Take advantage of the season when fresh corn is plentiful to create this cookout classic. This uses a lot of corn and is a nice alternative to corn on the cob.

INGREDIENTS

4 CUPS FRESH OR FROZEN LIMA BEANS

12 EARS OF CORN, SHUCKED AND RINSED

½ LB. THICK-CUT BACON

3 TABLESPOONS UNSALTED BUTTER

1 CUP WATER, AT ROOM TEMPERATURE

1 CUP WHOLE MILK, PLUS MORE AS NEEDED

KOSHER SALT AND FRESHLY GROUND BLACK PEPPER, TO TASTE

3 TABLESPOONS ALL-PURPOSE FLOUR

1 CUP CHERRY TOMATOES, HALVED

DIRECTIONS

1. Bring a medium pot of salted water to a boil over high heat. Add the lima beans and reduce the heat. Cook until they are al dente, about 5 minutes. Drain and set aside.

2. Standing each ear up in the middle of a large baking dish, use a sharp knife to cut down the sides and remove all the kernels. With the kernels off, take the blade of a dull knife and press it along each side of the ears to "milk" the cob of its liquid. Discard the milked cobs.

3. Place the bacon in a nonstick skillet and cook over medium heat until it is crispy, about 8 minutes. Transfer to a paper towel–lined plate and let it drain. When cool enough to handle, chop the bacon into bite-sized pieces.

4. Place a 12-inch cast-iron skillet over medium heat. When hot, lower the heat and add the butter so it melts slowly. When melted, add the corn kernels and "milk" from the cobs and stir to coat the kernels with the butter. Increase the heat to medium-high and add the water and whole milk. Bring to a boil, while stirring constantly, and then reduce heat to low. Add the lima beans, salt, and pepper.

5. Add the flour, cherry tomatoes, and bacon pieces to the skillet, stir to incorporate, and cook over low heat until the sauce thickens. If it gets too thick, add some more whole milk. Serve hot.

TIP: You'll want to freeze some of this to enjoy in the dead of winter. It's easy. Allow the succotash to cool, put it in airtight containers, being sure to push all the air out, seal the container, and place in the freezer. Put the date it was cooked on the container so you remember.

Edamame Succotash

YIELD: **4 TO 6 SERVINGS**

ACTIVE TIME: **5 MINUTES**

TOTAL TIME: **20 MINUTES**

Everyone knows that "succotash" is fun to say, but many have never tried the dish that has proven to be such a lexical delight. Maybe that's because of the divisive lima beans that feature in traditional preparations. Sub in the protein-rich and bright edamame and this side dish will be a welcome sight at any picnic or barbecue.

INGREDIENTS

4 SLICES OF THICK-CUT BACON

1 RED ONION, MINCED

KERNELS FROM 5 EARS OF CORN (ABOUT 4 CUPS)

1 RED BELL PEPPER, SEEDED AND DICED

1 CUP CANNED BLACK BEANS, DRAINED (OPTIONAL)

2 CUPS FRESH OR FROZEN EDAMAME

1 TABLESPOON UNSALTED BUTTER

SALT AND PEPPER, TO TASTE

1 TABLESPOON MINCED FRESH MARJORAM OR OREGANO

½ CUP CHOPPED FRESH BASIL

DIRECTIONS

1. Place a 12-inch cast-iron skillet over medium heat, then add the bacon and cook until crispy, about 8 minutes. Remove from the pan and place on a paper towel–lined plate to drain. When it is cool enough to handle, crumble into bite-sized pieces.

2. Wipe the excess drippings from the skillet and add the onion. Cook over medium-high heat until it has softened, about 5 minutes. Add the corn, bell pepper, black beans (if using), and edamame and cook, while stirring often, until the corn is tender and bright yellow, about 4 minutes.

3. Add the butter and stir until it has melted and everything is evenly coated. Season with salt and pepper.

4. Add the marjoram or oregano, basil, and crumbled bacon, stir to incorporate, and serve.

Green Beans with Bacon

YIELD: **4 SERVINGS**

ACTIVE TIME: **10 MINUTES**

TOTAL TIME: **15 MINUTES**

As contemporary culture continually asserts, you can never go wrong with bacon. Smoky, salty, and buttery, the balance of flavors it possesses is unmatched. Here it is charged with lifting green beans to transcendent heights, a task it handles beautifully.

INGREDIENTS

6 SLICES OF UNCURED BACON

2 CUPS TRIMMED GREEN BEANS

SALT AND PEPPER, TO TASTE

DIRECTIONS

1. Place a cast-iron skillet over medium heat for 5 minutes, until it is hot. Add the bacon and cook until it is browned, about 6 minutes. Transfer to a paper towel–lined plate to drain. When cool enough to handle, crumble into bite-sized pieces.

2. Remove all but 2 tablespoons of the bacon drippings from the skillet. Add the green beans and sauté, while tossing to coat, for about 4 minutes. The green beans should be bright green and just tender. Remove from the skillet and season with salt and pepper.

3. Sprinkle the crumbled bacon on top and serve.

Ratatouille

YIELD: **4 SERVINGS**

ACTIVE TIME: **40 MINUTES**

TOTAL TIME: **2 HOURS**

There are variations on this dish—some insist that zucchini is a necessary ingredient—but this recipe, which makes a simple, filling meal, calls for just eggplant, peppers, and tomatoes (and garlic, of course).

INGREDIENTS

⅓ CUP OLIVE OIL, PLUS MORE AS NEEDED

6 GARLIC CLOVES, MINCED

1 EGGPLANT, TRIMMED AND CUT INTO BITE-SIZED CUBES

2 BELL PEPPERS, SEEDED AND DICED

4 TOMATOES, SEEDED AND CHOPPED

SALT AND PEPPER, TO TASTE

DIRECTIONS

1. Heat half of the olive oil in a 12-inch cast-iron skillet over medium-high heat. Add the garlic and eggplant and cook, while stirring, until the pieces are coated with oil and just starting to sizzle, about 2 minutes. Reduce the heat slightly, add the peppers and remaining oil, and stir to combine. With the heat on medium, cover the skillet and let cook, stirring every few minutes to be sure vegetables aren't sticking to the bottom of the pan. If the mix seems too dry, add a little more olive oil. As the eggplant softens, the dish will regain moisture.

2. After about 15 minutes, when the eggplant and peppers are nearly soft, add the tomatoes and stir to combine. With the lid off, continue to cook the ratatouille, stirring occasionally, until the eggplant and peppers are soft and the tomatoes are wilted. Remove the skillet from heat, season with salt and pepper, and allow to sit for at least 1 hour. Reheat before serving.

VARIATION: If you want to make this with zucchini, choose a small one, and cut it into thin half-moons. Add the zucchini with the peppers.

CHAPTER 8

DESSERTS

We all know how blissful dessert can be, but did you know
how much more delicious some of your favorites can be when
made in cast iron? Turn the page to discover a world of buttery,
sweet, and decadent possibilities, like Boozy Pecan Pie
(see page 220) and Summer Crisp (see page 245).

Flaky Pastry Crust

This is a traditional piecrust recipe, and while it's tempting to take a shortcut and use a mix or even a premade crust, there truly is nothing as delicious as a crust made from scratch. Once you get the hang of it, you'll find making the crust as enjoyable and therapeutic as indulging in the pie.

YIELD: **12-INCH CRUST**

ACTIVE TIME: **30 MINUTES**

TOTAL TIME: **2 TO 3 HOURS**

INGREDIENTS

2½ CUPS ALL-PURPOSE FLOUR, PLUS MORE FOR DUSTING

1¼ TEASPOONS SALT

¼ CUP VEGETABLE SHORTENING

1 STICK OF UNSALTED BUTTER, CHILLED AND CUT INTO SMALL PIECES, PLUS 1 TABLESPOON FOR GREASING THE SKILLET

6-8 TABLESPOONS COLD WATER

DIRECTIONS

---

1. In a large bowl, combine the flour and salt. Add the shortening, and using a fork, work it in until the mixture forms a very coarse meal. Add the stick of butter and work it into the dough with a pastry blender or your fingers until the butter is incorporated. Don't overwork the dough; there can be chunks of butter in it. Add 4 tablespoons cold water to start and, using your hands or a fork, work the dough, adding additional tablespoons of water until the dough just holds together when you gather it in your hands.

2. Working on a lightly floured surface, gather the dough and form it into a solid ball. Separate into equal parts and form into disks. Wrap each tightly in plastic wrap and refrigerate for 30 to 60 minutes. Dough can be refrigerated for a couple of days or frozen for a couple of months.

3. Take the dough out of the refrigerator to allow it to warm up a bit, but work with it cold. Put the refrigerated dough on a lightly floured surface and, with a lightly dusted rolling pin, flatten the dough into 2 circles, working to extend each to a 12-inch round.

4. Grease a 12-inch cast-iron skillet with the remaining tablespoon of butter.

Continued...

5. Carefully position the crust in the skillet so it is evenly distributed, pressing it in lightly and allowing the dough to extend over the side.

6. If making a single-crust pie, crimp the edges as desired. If filling and adding a top crust, leave the extra dough so it can be crimped with the top crust. Fill the pie as directed, and then roll out the top crust so it is just bigger than the diameter of the top of the skillet. For an extra-flaky pastry crust, refrigerate the assembled pie for about 30 minutes before baking.

7. When ready to bake, cut a slit or hole in the middle of the top crust for heat and water vapor to escape. Brush the crust with milk, which will turn it a nice brown color. Bake as directed.

Baked Crust

YIELD: **12-INCH CRUST**

ACTIVE TIME: **20 MINUTES**

TOTAL TIME: **2 HOURS**

This classic crust is fast and easy to put together, and the result is delicious.

INGREDIENTS

1¼ CUPS ALL-PURPOSE FLOUR, PLUS MORE FOR DUSTING

¼ TEASPOON SALT

1 STICK OF UNSALTED BUTTER, CHILLED AND CUT INTO SMALL PIECES, PLUS 1 TABLESPOON FOR GREASING THE SKILLET

4-6 TABLESPOONS ICE WATER

DIRECTIONS

1. In a large bowl, combine the flour and salt. Add the stick of butter and work it into the flour mixture with a pastry blender or 2 knives until the dough resembles coarse meal. Add 3 tablespoons cold water to start, and, using your hands or a fork, work the dough, adding additional tablespoons of water until the dough just holds together when you gather it in your hands.

2. Working on a lightly floured surface, gather the dough and form it into a solid ball or disk. Wrap tightly in plastic wrap and refrigerate for about an hour. The dough can be refrigerated for a couple of days or frozen for a couple of months.

3. Preheat the oven to 450°F. Take the dough out of the refrigerator to allow it to warm up a bit, but work with it cold. Put the refrigerated dough on a lightly floured surface, and, with a lightly dusted rolling pin, flatten the dough into a circle, working to extend it to a 12-inch round.

4. Grease a 12-inch cast-iron skillet with the remaining tablespoon of butter.

5. Carefully position the crust in the skillet so it is evenly distributed, pressing it in lightly. Crimp the edges. Use a fork to prick the crust on the bottom and sides. Line with foil or parchment paper and fill with uncooked rice as a weight.

6. Bake for 10 to 12 minutes, until lightly browned. Transfer to a wire rack to cool before filling.

Graham Cracker Crust

YIELD: **10-INCH CRUST**

ACTIVE TIME: **20 MINUTES**

TOTAL TIME: **45 MINUTES**

You can crush graham crackers to make this crust, or you can purchase graham cracker crumbs in the baked goods aisle of your grocery store. Either works, as the cracker is held together with butter and sugar. There are so many fillings that complement the flavor and texture of a graham cracker crust, so be sure to experiment and enjoy.

INGREDIENTS

1½ CUPS GRAHAM CRACKER CRUMBS

2 TABLESPOONS SUGAR

1 TABLESPOON MAPLE SYRUP

5 TABLESPOONS UNSALTED BUTTER, MELTED, PLUS 1 TABLESPOON AT ROOM TEMPERATURE FOR GREASING THE SKILLET

DIRECTIONS

1. Preheat the oven to 375°F.

2. In a large bowl, add the graham cracker crumbs and sugar and stir to combine. Add the maple syrup and melted butter and stir to thoroughly combine.

3. Liberally grease a 10-inch cast-iron skillet with the tablespoon of room-temperature butter. Pour the dough into the skillet and lightly press into shape. Line with aluminum foil and fill with uncooked rice. Bake for 10 to 12 minutes, until golden.

4. Allow to cool on a wire rack before filling.

Classic Blueberry Pie

YIELD: **6 TO 8 SERVINGS**

ACTIVE TIME: **1 HOUR**

TOTAL TIME: **2 HOURS**

An incredibly easy way to capture the brief glory that is blueberry season. It's summer in a slice!

INGREDIENTS

4 CUPS FRESH OR FROZEN BLUEBERRIES

1 TABLESPOON FRESH LEMON JUICE

1 CUP GRANULATED SUGAR, PLUS 2 TABLESPOONS

3 TABLESPOONS ALL-PURPOSE FLOUR

1 STICK OF UNSALTED BUTTER

1 CUP LIGHT BROWN SUGAR

2 FLAKY PASTRY CRUSTS (SEE PAGE 214)

1 EGG WHITE

DIRECTIONS

1. Preheat the oven to 350°F.

2. If using frozen blueberries, it's not necessary to thaw them completely. Put the blueberries in a large bowl and add the lemon juice, 1 cup of granulated sugar, and flour. Stir to combine.

3. Put a 10-inch cast-iron skillet over medium heat and melt the butter in it. Add the brown sugar and cook, while stirring constantly, until the brown sugar is dissolved, 1 or 2 minutes. Remove pan from heat.

4. Gently place one crust over the butter-and-sugar mixture. Fill with the blueberries and place the other crust over the blueberries, crimping the edges together.

5. Brush the top crust with the egg white and then sprinkle the remaining granulated sugar over it. Cut 4 or 5 slits in the middle.

6. Put the skillet in the oven and bake for 50 to 60 minutes, until the pie is golden brown and bubbly. Cover the outermost edge with aluminum foil in the last 10 minutes of baking to prevent it from burning.

7. Remove from the oven and allow to cool before serving.

TIP: If you feel like adding a decorative touch to your pie, cut your second crust into strips and lay them across the top to make a picture-perfect lattice crust.

Cherry Pie

YIELD: **4 TO 6 SERVINGS**

ACTIVE TIME: **30 MINUTES**

TOTAL TIME: **1 HOUR AND 30 MINUTES**

Nothing heralds the true start of spring like cherry blossoms, and what better way to showcase that beautiful display than using the resulting fruits to make an irresistible pie?

INGREDIENTS

4 CUPS CHERRIES (DARK OR RAINIER PREFERRED), PITTED

2 CUPS SUGAR

2 TABLESPOONS FRESH LEMON JUICE

3 TABLESPOONS CORNSTARCH

1 TABLESPOON WATER

¼ TEASPOON ALMOND EXTRACT

2 FLAKY PASTRY CRUSTS (SEE PAGE 214)

1 EGG, BEATEN

DIRECTIONS

1. Preheat oven to 350°F. Place the cherries, sugar, and lemon juice in a saucepan and cook, while stirring occasionally, over medium heat until the mixture is syrupy.

2. Combine the cornstarch and water in a small bowl and stir this mixture into the saucepan. Reduce heat to low and cook, while stirring, until the mixture is thick. Remove from heat, add the almond extract, and let cool.

3. When the cherry mixture has cooled, place the bottom crust in a greased cast-iron skillet and pour the cherry mixture into the crust. Top with the other crust, make a few slits in the top, and brush the top crust with the beaten egg.

4. Place the pie in the oven and bake until the top crust is golden brown, about 45 minutes. Remove and let cool before serving.

Boozy Pecan Pie

YIELD: **8 TO 10 SERVINGS**

ACTIVE TIME: **45 MINUTES**

TOTAL TIME: **2 HOURS**

Here's another step up in the pecan pie department. If you're looking to make a pie that will have your guests raving about your cooking, this is the one!

INGREDIENTS

1½ CUPS PECANS

1 FLAKY PASTRY CRUST (SEE PAGE 214)

6 OZ. SEMISWEET CHOCOLATE CHIPS

1 CUP DARK CORN SYRUP

⅓ CUP GRANULATED SUGAR

½ CUP FIRMLY PACKED LIGHT BROWN SUGAR

¼ CUP BOURBON

4 LARGE EGGS

4 TABLESPOONS UNSALTED BUTTER, MELTED

2 TEASPOONS VANILLA EXTRACT

½ TEASPOON TABLE SALT

DIRECTIONS

1. Preheat the oven to 350°F. Spread the pecan pieces on a baking sheet in a single layer. Bake for 6 to 10 minutes, checking often to make sure they don't burn. When fragrant, remove from oven and let cool. Chop pecans into small pieces and set aside.

2. Reduce oven temperature to 325°F.

3. Working with the crust in a 12-inch cast-iron skillet, sprinkle the toasted pecan pieces and chocolate chips evenly onto the crust.

4. In a saucepan over medium heat, combine the corn syrup, granulated sugar, light brown sugar, and bourbon. Stir to combine and cook, while stirring constantly, until the mixture just comes to a boil. Remove from heat.

5. In a large bowl, whisk the eggs until thoroughly combined. Add the melted butter, vanilla, and salt and whisk to combine. Add about ¼ of the sugar-and-bourbon mixture to the egg mixture, whisking briskly to combine so the eggs don't curdle or cook. When thoroughly combined, continue to add the hot liquid to the egg mixture in small amounts, whisking to combine thoroughly after each addition until all of it is incorporated. Pour this mixture over the nuts and chocolate pieces and shake the skillet gently to distribute evenly.

6. Put the skillet in the oven and bake for 1 hour or until a knife inserted toward the middle comes out clean. If the edge of the crust becomes overly brown, remove the skillet from the oven and put aluminum foil over the exposed crust until the filling is set. Remove the skillet from the oven and allow to cool completely before serving.

Chocolate & Salted Pistachio Pudding Pie

YIELD: **6 TO 8 SERVINGS**

ACTIVE TIME: **1 HOUR**

TOTAL TIME: **2 TO 24 HOURS**

So easy to make, so good, and so colorful. Kids love this one. And guess what? So do adults.

INGREDIENTS

7 TABLESPOONS UNSALTED BUTTER, MELTED

8 OZ. VANILLA WAFER COOKIES, CRUSHED

2 OZ. SEMISWEET CHOCOLATE CHIPS

¼ CUP SWEETENED CONDENSED MILK

1 CUP SALTED, SHELLED PISTACHIO PIECES, PLUS MORE FOR TOPPING

2 (3.4 OZ.) BOXES OF INSTANT PISTACHIO PUDDING MIX

2 CUPS WHOLE MILK

1 CUP COOL WHIP OR WHIPPED CREAM, FOR TOPPING (OPTIONAL)

DIRECTIONS

1. Warm a 10-inch cast-iron skillet over low heat and then place 1 tablespoon of the butter into it.

2. In a large bowl, mix the cookie crumbs with the remaining butter until combined. Carefully remove the cast-iron skillet from the heat and press the cookie mixture into the bottom of the pan to form a crust. Allow to cool and set.

3. In a small microwave-safe bowl, microwave the chocolate in 15-second increments, removing to stir after each, until just melted. Stir in the sweetened condensed milk.

4. Pour the chocolate mixture over the crust. Sprinkle with half of the salted pistachio pieces. Refrigerate for about 30 minutes.

5. In a large bowl, whisk together the pudding mix and milk for about 3 minutes, until the mixture is smooth and thick. Put the pudding into the crust and spread evenly. Sprinkle with remaining pistachios. Add a layer of whipped topping, if desired.

6. Cover with plastic wrap and refrigerate for at least 1 hour and up to a day. When ready to serve, remove plastic wrap and sprinkle with additional salted pistachio pieces.

Lemon Meringue Pie

YIELD: **6 TO 8 SERVINGS**

ACTIVE TIME: **1 HOUR**

TOTAL TIME: **1 HOUR AND 30 MINUTES**

To really drive home the wonderful lemon flavor of this pie be sure to use fresh lemon juice, not the stuff that comes in a bottle. It makes a huge difference.

INGREDIENTS

⅓ CUP CORNSTARCH

1½ CUPS SUGAR

¼ TEASPOON SALT, PLUS A PINCH

1½ CUPS WATER

ZEST OF 1 LEMON

½ CUP FRESH LEMON JUICE

4 EGGS, SEPARATED

1 TABLESPOON UNSALTED BUTTER

1 BAKED CRUST (SEE PAGE 216)

DIRECTIONS

1. Preheat the oven to 400°F.

2. In a saucepan, combine the cornstarch, 1 cup of the sugar, and pinch of salt. Whisk to combine. Stir in the water, lemon zest, and lemon juice. Cook over medium heat, stirring constantly, until mixture comes to a boil. Remove the saucepan from heat.

3. Place the egg yolks in a bowl and add a spoonful of the hot lemon mixture. Stir rapidly to combine so the eggs don't cook or curdle. Add another spoonful of the lemon mixture and repeat. Transfer the tempered egg yolks to the saucepan and stir constantly to combine well.

4. Cook over medium heat, while stirring. Add the butter. Stir until butter is completely melted and the mixture has thickened, about 3 minutes.

5. Working with the crust in a 10-inch cast-iron skillet, transfer the filling into the piecrust.

6. In a large bowl, beat the egg whites and the remaining salt with an electric mixer on high until soft peaks form. Continue to beat, adding the remaining sugar 2 tablespoons at a time until all the sugar has been incorporated and stiff peaks start to form.

7. Spoon the meringue onto the lemon filling and spread to cover evenly.

8. Put the skillet in the oven for about 10 minutes, until the meringue is just golden.

9. Remove skillet and allow to cool completely before serving.

Sweet Lemon Tart

YIELD: **6 TO 8 SERVINGS**

ACTIVE TIME: **30 MINUTES**

TOTAL TIME: **1 HOUR**

Lemons are like sunshine—they brighten everything! Very thinly sliced lemons sit atop a lemon-drenched custard to make a dessert whose flavor shines from the first bite to the last.

INGREDIENTS

1 (14 OZ.) CAN OF SWEETENED CONDENSED MILK

½ CUP FRESH LEMON JUICE

4 LARGE EGG YOLKS

1 TABLESPOON VANILLA EXTRACT

1 GRAHAM CRACKER CRUST (SEE PAGE 217)

1 LEMON, SEEDED AND SLICED VERY THIN

DIRECTIONS

1. Preheat the oven to 325°F.

2. In a medium bowl, combine the condensed milk, lemon juice, egg yolks, and vanilla. Working with the crust in a 10-inch cast-iron skillet, pour the filling into the crust. Top with the very thin slices of lemon, arranged in a decorative pattern.

3. Put the skillet in the oven and bake for about 15 to 20 minutes, until the liquid has set into a soft custard.

4. Remove the skillet from the oven and allow to cool completely before serving.

French Apple Tart

YIELD: **6 TO 8 SERVINGS**

ACTIVE TIME: **1 HOUR**

TOTAL TIME: **2 TO 24 HOURS**

Cast-iron skillets caramelize fruits to perfection. This recipe is the quintessential example. It's what the French call **tarte Tatin***, and for them it's a national treasure.*

INGREDIENTS

1 CUP ALL-PURPOSE FLOUR, PLUS MORE FOR DUSTING

½ TEASPOON SALT

1½ CUPS SUGAR, PLUS 1 TABLESPOON

2 STICKS UNSALTED BUTTER, CUT INTO SMALL PIECES

3 TABLESPOONS ICE WATER

8 APPLES, PEELED, CORED, AND SLICED

DIRECTIONS

1. To make the pastry, whisk together the flour, salt, and 1 tablespoon of sugar in a large bowl. Using your fingers, work 6 tablespoons of the butter into the flour mixture until you have coarse clumps. Sprinkle the ice water over the mixture and continue to work it with your hands until the dough just holds together. Shape it into a ball, wrap it in plastic wrap, and refrigerate it for at least 1 hour or overnight.

2. The tart starts in a 12-inch cast-iron skillet. Place the remaining pieces of butter evenly over the bottom of the skillet, then sprinkle the remaining sugar evenly over everything. Next, start placing the apple slices in a circular pattern, starting at the edge of the pan and working in. The slices should overlap and face the same direction. Place either 1 or 2 slices in the center when finished working around the outside. As the tart bakes, the slices will slide down a bit.

3. Place the skillet on the stove and turn the heat to high. Cook until the juices in the pan are a deep amber color, about 10 minutes. Remove from heat and turn the apples over. Place the skillet back over high heat, cook for another 5 minutes, and then turn off the heat.

4. Preheat the oven to 400°F and position a rack in the center.

Continued...

5. Take the chilled dough out of the refrigerator and, working on a lightly floured surface, roll it out into a circle just big enough to cover the skillet (about 12 to 14 inches). Taking care not to burn your fingers on the hot skillet, drape the pastry over the apples and pinch it in around the sides.

6. Put the skillet in the oven and bake for about 25 minutes, until the pastry is golden brown.

7. Remove the skillet from the oven and allow to cool for about 5 minutes. Find a plate that is an inch or 2 larger than the top of the skillet and place it over the top. You will be inverting the tart onto the plate. Be sure to use oven mitts or secure pot holders, as the skillet will be hot.

8. Holding the plate tightly against the top of the skillet, turn the skillet over so the plate is now on the bottom. If some of the apples are stuck to the bottom, gently remove them and place them on the tart. Allow to cool a few more minutes, or set aside until ready to serve. The tart is best served warm.

Peach Galette

YIELD: **6 TO 8 SERVINGS**

ACTIVE TIME: **45 MINUTES**

TOTAL TIME: **1 HOUR AND 30 MINUTES**

When peaches are ripe in the summer, this is a super-simple way to turn them into a great dessert. Smearing some peach jam on the crust before adding the fruit will intensify the flavor, and if you want something a little more "adult," consider adding some Amaretto or bourbon to the jam.

INGREDIENTS

1 FLAKY PASTRY CRUST
(SEE PAGE 214)

3 CUPS FRESH PEACHES, PEELED
(OPTIONAL), PITTED, AND SLICED

½ CUP SUGAR, PLUS 1 TABLESPOON

JUICE OF ½ LEMON

3 TABLESPOONS CORNSTARCH

PINCH OF SALT

1 TEASPOON AMARETTO OR
BOURBON (OPTIONAL)

2 TABLESPOONS PEACH JAM

1 EGG, BEATEN

DIRECTIONS

1. Preheat the oven to 400°F.

2. When rolling out the crust, keep in mind that it should be slightly larger than the bottom of the pan so that it can be folded over. Place the crust in a greased 10-inch cast-iron skillet.

3. In a large bowl, mix the peaches with the ½ cup of sugar, lemon juice, cornstarch, and salt. Stir well to coat all the fruit.

4. If using the Amaretto or bourbon, mix it with the jam in a small bowl before brushing or smearing the jam over the center of the crust.

5. Place the peaches in a mound in the center of the crust. Fold the edge of the crust over to cover about 1 inch of filling. Brush the crust with the beaten egg and sprinkle it with the remaining sugar.

6. Put the skillet in the oven and bake until the filling is bubbly, which is necessary for it to thicken, about 35 to 40 minutes.

7. Remove the skillet from the oven and let cool before serving.

Plum Galette

YIELD: **4 TO 6 SERVINGS**

ACTIVE TIME: **40 MINUTES**

TOTAL TIME: **1 HOUR AND 30 MINUTES**

Here's another summer fruit–laden treat that is so easy to put together and tastes great! The flavor of the plums is definitely enhanced by the jam, and the whole thing is sublime when topped with ice cream and roasted and salted pumpkin seeds.

INGREDIENTS

1 FLAKY PASTRY CRUST
(SEE PAGE 214)

3 CUPS FRESH PLUMS, PITTED
AND SLICED

½ CUP SUGAR, PLUS 1 TABLESPOON

JUICE OF ½ LEMON

3 TABLESPOONS CORNSTARCH

PINCH OF SALT

2 TABLESPOONS BLACKBERRY JAM

1 EGG, BEATEN

DIRECTIONS

1. Preheat the oven to 400°F.

2. When rolling out the crust, keep in mind that it should be slightly larger than the bottom of the pan so that it can be folded over. Place the crust in a greased 10-inch cast-iron skillet.

3. In a large bowl, mix the plums with ½ cup of the sugar, lemon juice, cornstarch, and salt. Stir well to coat all the fruit.

4. Brush or smear the jam over the center of the crust. Place the plums in a mound in the center. Fold the edges of the crust over to cover about 1 inch of the filling. Brush the crust with the beaten egg and sprinkle it with the remaining sugar.

5. Put the skillet in the oven and bake until the filling is bubbly, which is necessary for it to thicken, about 35 to 40 minutes.

6. Remove the skillet from the oven and let cool before serving.

Pineapple Upside-Down Cake

YIELD: **8 TO 10 SERVINGS**

ACTIVE TIME: **1 HOUR**

TOTAL TIME: **2 HOURS**

This is another recipe that is cooked to perfection in a cast-iron skillet. In 1925, Dole sponsored a pineapple recipe contest, promising to publish winning recipes in a book. The company received over 50,000 recipes, and over 2,000 of them were for a version of this cake. It's been a classic of American cooking ever since.

INGREDIENTS

1 STICK OF UNSALTED BUTTER,
½ AT ROOM TEMPERATURE,
½ CHILLED

1 (20 OZ.) CAN OF PINEAPPLE
RINGS, WITH THE JUICE

½ CUP DARK BROWN SUGAR

MARASCHINO CHERRIES,
AS NEEDED (OPTIONAL)

1 CUP LIGHT BROWN SUGAR

2 EGGS

1 CUP BUTTERMILK

1 TEASPOON VANILLA EXTRACT

1½ CUPS ALL-PURPOSE FLOUR

1½ TEASPOONS BAKING POWDER

½ TEASPOON SALT

DIRECTIONS

1. Preheat the oven to 350°F.

2. Place a 10-inch cast-iron skillet over medium-high heat. Add the room-temperature butter, the juice from the can of pineapples, and the dark brown sugar. Stir continuously while the sugar melts, and continue stirring until the liquid boils and starts to thicken. Cook until the sauce darkens and gains the consistency of caramel.

3. Remove from heat and place the pineapple rings in the liquid, working from the outside in. If adding cherries, place a cherry in the center of each ring. Put the skillet in the oven while preparing the batter.

4. Beat the 4 tablespoons cold butter and light brown sugar with an electric mixer until light and creamy. Beat in the eggs one at a time, making sure the first is thoroughly incorporated before adding the next. Add the buttermilk and vanilla extract.

5. In a small bowl, whisk together the flour, baking powder, and salt. Combine the dry and wet mixtures and stir until combined but not overly smooth.

Continued...

6. Remove the skillet from the oven and pour the batter over the pineapple rings. Return to the oven and bake for 45 minutes, until the cake is golden and a knife inserted in the center of the cake comes out clean.

7. Remove from the oven and let rest for about 10 minutes.

8. Find a plate that is an inch or two larger than the top of the skillet and place it over the top. You will be inverting the cake onto the plate.

Be sure to use oven mitts or secure pot holders, as the skillet will be hot. Holding the plate tightly against the top of the skillet, turn the skillet over so the plate is on the bottom. If some of the pineapple is stuck to the bottom of the skillet, gently remove it and place it on the cake.

9. Allow to cool a few more minutes, or set aside until ready to serve. The cake is best served warm.

Dutch Apple Baby

This is a classic cast-iron skillet recipe for a pastry that puffs up in the oven.

YIELD: **4 SERVINGS**

ACTIVE TIME: **45 MINUTES**

TOTAL TIME: **1 HOUR AND 15 MINUTES**

INGREDIENTS

2 FIRM, SEMI-TART APPLES (MUTSU OR GOLDEN DELICIOUS), PEELED AND CORED

4 TABLESPOONS UNSALTED BUTTER

¼ CUP SUGAR, PLUS 3 TABLESPOONS

1 TABLESPOON CINNAMON

¾ CUP ALL-PURPOSE FLOUR

¼ TEASPOON SALT

¾ CUP WHOLE MILK

4 EGGS

1 TEASPOON VANILLA OR ALMOND EXTRACT

CONFECTIONERS' SUGAR, FOR DUSTING

DIRECTIONS

1. Preheat the oven to 425°F and position a rack in the middle.

2. Cut the apples into slices. Heat a 10-inch cast-iron skillet over medium-high heat. Add the butter and apples and cook, while stirring, for 3 to 4 minutes, until the apples soften. Add the ¼ cup of sugar and cinnamon and continue cooking for another 3 or 4 minutes. Distribute the apples evenly over the bottom of the skillet and remove from heat.

3. In a large bowl, mix the remaining sugar, flour, and salt together. In a smaller bowl, whisk together the milk, eggs, and vanilla or almond extract. Add the wet ingredients to the dry ingredients and stir to combine. Pour the batter over the apples.

4. Place the skillet in the oven and bake for 15 to 20 minutes, until the "baby" is puffy and browned on the top.

5. Remove the skillet from the oven and allow to cool for a few minutes. Run a knife along the edge of the skillet to loosen the dessert. Put a plate over the skillet and, using oven mitts or pot holders, flip the skillet over so the dessert is transferred to the plate. Serve warm with a dusting of confectioners' sugar.

The Best Skillet Brownies

YIELD: **6 TO 8 SERVINGS**

ACTIVE TIME: **40 MINUTES**

TOTAL TIME: **1 HOUR AND 30 MINUTES**

If you're serious about brownies, you'll love this recipe. When shopping for the ingredients, remember that the better the chocolate, the better the taste and texture of the brownie. What gets baked up in the cast-iron skillet is a gooey yet crunchy confection that is heaven in every bite. Don't even slice them up—serve them right out of the skillet (when cool enough). Just be sure to have friends and family around when you do, as you may be tempted to eat the whole brownie by yourself.

INGREDIENTS

10 TABLESPOONS UNSALTED BUTTER

½ LB. SEMISWEET CHOCOLATE, COARSELY CHOPPED

1 CUP SUGAR

3 EGGS, AT ROOM TEMPERATURE

1 TEASPOON VANILLA EXTRACT

½ CUP ALL-PURPOSE FLOUR, PLUS 2 TABLESPOONS

2 TABLESPOONS UNSWEETENED COCOA POWDER

¼ TEASPOON SALT

1 CUP SEMISWEET CHOCOLATE CHIPS

VANILLA ICE CREAM, FOR SERVING (OPTIONAL)

DIRECTIONS

1. Preheat the oven to 350°F.

2. In a microwave-safe bowl, microwave 9 tablespoons of the butter and chopped chocolate pieces together, cooking in 15-second increments and stirring after each, until the butter and chocolate are just melted together and smooth.

3. In a large bowl, add the sugar and eggs and whisk to combine. Add the vanilla and stir to combine. Working in batches, start mixing the melted chocolate into the mixture, stirring vigorously to combine after each addition. In a small bowl, mix the flour, cocoa powder, and salt. Gently fold the dry mixture into the chocolate mixture. Next, fold in the chocolate chips.

4. Over medium heat, melt the remaining butter in a 10-inch cast-iron skillet. When melted, pour in the batter. Place the skillet in the oven and bake for about 30 minutes or until a toothpick inserted in the center comes out with a few moist crumbs. It may need a couple more minutes, but be careful not to overbake this or you'll lose the gooeyness that makes these brownies so great. When the brownies are ready, remove the skillet from the oven and allow to cool for about 10 minutes.

Continued...

5.   Dig right in, or scoop into
     bowls and serve with your favorite ice cream.

VARIATION: To give the brownies a refreshing
zing, add 1½ teaspoon of peppermint extract and 1
cup of chopped York Peppermint Patties to the batter.

Giant Chocolate Chip Cookie

YIELD: **6 TO 8 SERVINGS**

ACTIVE TIME: **20 MINUTES**

TOTAL TIME: **45 MINUTES**

Yes, your cast-iron skillet is also a great baking sheet—just smaller, and with sides. So why not bake a giant cookie in it?

INGREDIENTS

2 STICKS OF UNSALTED BUTTER, AT ROOM TEMPERATURE

½ CUP GRANULATED SUGAR

1 CUP BROWN SUGAR

2 EGGS

2 TEASPOONS VANILLA EXTRACT

1 TEASPOON BAKING SODA

2 TEASPOONS HOT WATER (120°F)

½ TEASPOON SALT

2½ CUPS ALL-PURPOSE FLOUR

2 CUPS SEMISWEET CHOCOLATE CHIPS

ICE CREAM, FOR SERVING

DIRECTIONS

1. Preheat oven to 375°F. Place a 12-inch cast-iron skillet in the oven while making the batter.

2. In a large bowl, beat the butter and sugars together until light and fluffy. Add the eggs one at a time, being sure to combine each one thoroughly before proceeding to the next. Stir in the vanilla.

3. Dissolve the baking soda in the hot water and add to the batter with the salt. Stir in the flour and chocolate chips.

4. Remove the skillet from the oven and put the batter in it, smoothing the top with a rubber spatula.

5. Put the skillet in the oven and bake for about 15 minutes, until golden. Serve with ice cream.

Classic Shortbread

YIELD: **6 TO 8 SERVINGS**

ACTIVE TIME: **25 MINUTES**

TOTAL TIME: **1 HOUR**

Shortbread is wonderfully simple to prepare and so, so yummy. The butter shines through in each flaky bite. These wedges are the perfect late-afternoon pick-me-up when served with coffee, tea, or hot chocolate.

INGREDIENTS

1 CUP ALL-PURPOSE FLOUR, PLUS MORE FOR DUSTING

¼ TEASPOON SALT

¼ CUP SUGAR

1 STICK OF UNSALTED BUTTER, CHILLED

½ TEASPOON VANILLA EXTRACT

DIRECTIONS

1. Preheat the oven to 300°F. Place a 12-inch cast-iron skillet in the oven while making the dough.

2. In a large bowl, combine the flour, salt, and sugar, whisking to combine.

3. Cut the butter into slices and add to the flour mixture. The best way to work it into the flour is with your hands. As it starts to come together, add the vanilla extract. Work the mixture until it resembles coarse meal.

4. Gather the dough into a ball. On a lightly floured surface, roll it out into a circle that's just smaller than the surface of the skillet. Slice the round into 8 wedges.

5. Remove the skillet from the oven and place the wedges in it to recreate the circle of dough. Bake for about 45 minutes or until the shortbread is a pale golden color. Remove the skillet from the oven and allow to cool for about 10 minutes before transferring the cookies to a plate.

Walnut Bread Pudding

YIELD: **4 TO 6 SERVINGS**

ACTIVE TIME: **45 MINUTES**

TOTAL TIME: **2 HOURS**

If you want a super-simple, irresistible recipe for no-fail bread pudding, look no further. The addition of toasted walnut pieces sets this dish apart. The better the quality of the ice cream, the tastier the bread pudding will be and the better it will set up.

INGREDIENTS

½ CUP WALNUTS, CHOPPED

4 TABLESPOONS UNSALTED BUTTER

4 CUPS DAY-OLD BREAD PIECES

½ CUP RAISINS

2 EGGS

¼ CUP RUM

1 PINT OF VANILLA ICE CREAM, AT ROOM TEMPERATURE

DIRECTIONS

1. Place a 10-inch cast-iron skillet over medium-high heat. When hot, add the walnuts. Shake the walnuts in the skillet while they cook. You want them to toast but not brown or burn. This should take just a few minutes.

2. When toasted, transfer the walnuts to a plate and allow to cool.

3. Reduce heat to low, add the butter to the skillet, and let it melt. Add the bread pieces and raisins to the skillet and distribute evenly. Sprinkle the walnuts over the bread.

4. In a bowl, whisk the eggs and the rum together. Add the ice cream and stir just enough to combine. Pour this mixture over the bread and nuts. Shake the skillet gently to distribute the liquid evenly.

5. Cover with aluminum foil, put in a cool place, and allow the mixture to rest for about 30 minutes so that the bread cubes can soak up the liquid.

6. Preheat the oven to 350°F.

7. Uncover the skillet and bake until the bread pudding is set and the edges are slightly browned, about 40 minutes. Use pot holders or oven mitts to take the skillet out of the oven. Allow to cool for 5 to 10 minutes before serving.

VARIATION: Make a pretty and patriotic red, white, and blue bread pudding by substituting strawberry ice cream for the vanilla and sprinkling fresh or frozen blueberries over the bread pieces before the skillet goes in the oven.

Fall Fruit Crumble

YIELD: **4 TO 6 SERVINGS**

ACTIVE TIME: **30 MINUTES**

TOTAL TIME: **45 MINUTES**

The tart pop of the Cortland apples and the sweet softness of the red pears give this dish a wonderful balance, and adding freshly grated ginger to the topping really sets it apart.

INGREDIENTS

FOR THE TOPPING

½ CUP WHOLE WHEAT FLOUR

1 STICK OF UNSALTED BUTTER, CUT INTO SMALL PIECES

½ CUP OATS

½ CUP BROWN SUGAR

¼ CUP GRANULATED SUGAR

1 TABLESPOON GRATED GINGER

½ TEASPOON CINNAMON

½ TEASPOON NUTMEG

½ TEASPOON KOSHER SALT

FOR THE FILLING

2 TABLESPOONS UNSALTED BUTTER

PINCH OF KOSHER SALT

2 TABLESPOONS BROWN SUGAR

2 TABLESPOONS TAPIOCA STARCH OR CORNSTARCH

3 CORTLAND APPLES, PEELED, QUARTERED, AND CUT INTO 20 EVEN SLICES

Continued…

DIRECTIONS

1. To prepare the topping, place all of the ingredients in a large mixing bowl and use a fork to mash the butter and other ingredients together. Continue until the topping is a collection of pea-sized pieces. Place the bowl in the refrigerator.

2. To prepare the filling, preheat the oven to 350°F.

3. Place an 8-inch cast-iron skillet over medium heat. Add the butter. Place the salt, brown sugar, and tapioca starch or cornstarch in a bowl and stir to combine.

4. Once the butter has melted, put the apple slices in the pan in one even layer, working from the outside toward the center. Cook for 5 to 7 minutes.

5. Sprinkle half of the brown sugar mixture over the apples.

6. Utilizing the same technique you used for the apple slices, layer all of the pear slices in the skillet. Sprinkle the remaining brown sugar mixture on top. Top with any remaining apple slices.

7. Combine the vanilla extract, almond extract, and lemon juice in a bowl and pour over all of the fruit.

8. Remove the topping from the refrigerator and spread in an even layer on top of the fruit. Cover the skillet with foil, place in the oven, and bake for 15 minutes.

Continued…

3 RED PEARS, PEELED, QUARTERED, AND CUT INTO 16 EVEN SLICES

1 TABLESPOON VANILLA EXTRACT

1 TABLESPOON ALMOND EXTRACT

JUICE OF ½ LEMON

ICE CREAM, FOR SERVING (OPTIONAL)

WHIPPED CREAM, FOR SERVING (OPTIONAL)

9. Remove the foil and bake for another 20 minutes.

10. If you would like the crisp to set, turn the oven off and open the door slightly. Let the skillet rest in the oven for another 20 minutes. Or remove the skillet, top the crisp with your favorite ice cream or whipped cream, and serve.

Summer Crisp

This magnificent combo traditionally appears in a pie, but this crisp allows you to enjoy it without all of the fuss.

YIELD: **4 SERVINGS**

ACTIVE TIME: **30 MINUTES**

TOTAL TIME: **1 HOUR**

INGREDIENTS

1½ CUPS CHOPPED RHUBARB

1½ CUPS HULLED AND SLICED STRAWBERRIES

2 TABLESPOONS GRANULATED SUGAR

⅓ CUP ALL-PURPOSE FLOUR, PLUS 2 TEASPOONS

4 TABLESPOONS UNSALTED BUTTER, CHILLED AND CUT INTO PIECES

¼ CUP DARK BROWN SUGAR

¾ CUP QUICK-COOKING OATS

¼ CUP CHOPPED HAZELNUTS (OPTIONAL)

WHIPPED CREAM, FOR SERVING (OPTIONAL)

ICE CREAM, FOR SERVING (OPTIONAL)

DIRECTIONS

1. Preheat the oven to 450°F.

2. In a bowl, combine the rhubarb pieces, strawberries, granulated sugar, and the 2 teaspoons of flour and toss to coat the fruit. Transfer to a 10-inch cast-iron skillet.

3. In another bowl, add the butter and brown sugar and work the mixture with a fork or pastry blender. Add the oats, hazelnuts (if using), and remaining flour and continue to work the mixture until it is a coarse meal. Sprinkle it over the fruit in the skillet.

4. Put the skillet in the oven and bake for about 30 minutes, until the topping is golden and the fruit is bubbly. Serve warm with whipped cream or ice cream.

CHAPTER 9

CAST-IRON CARE & KEEPING

Cast iron is the original nonstick cookware.
But whether you are using a pre-seasoned pan or a
vintage one, some care and keeping are called for in order to
maintain that nonstick quality. Luckily, it really isn't very hard, and
a little effort at the start of your relationship with a piece of cast-iron
cookware will save you a great deal of time in the long run. Not only
will it be conditioned to help you make the best food possible,
it'll be kept in tip-top condition so you can pass it along
to a friend or family member one day.

SEASONING CAST-IRON COOKWARE

A cast-iron pan is metal that has been poured into a mold and formed into a shape that allows you to cook food, hence why they are called cast-iron pans. Across the world, in every culture, humans have cooked in metal vessels that can withstand direct heat since we figured out how to extract metal from the earth. At first, they were rudimentary cauldrons, but over time they evolved into myriad shapes and sizes. For the most part, once the basic and most necessary shapes were created, the innovation in this field ended. Today, we better understand the science and the benefits of casting cookware, but for the most part nothing has changed in the last few hundred years. So, you have this pan. It's made from a raw material that needs to be seasoned to create a nonstick coating that acts as a defense against rusting. Many people have decided that the coating process and the maintenance of the seasoning is somehow difficult. It isn't. It's simple. What makes it complicated is that the general directions can be very detailed. But as with anything, it's better to have more information than not enough. The steps to seasoning your new cast-iron cookware are simple:

1   Wash it with warm, soapy water, using an abrasive sponge to really scrub it. If it just came from the store, it should be relatively clean, but you want to make sure there is no dust or debris.

2   Dry the pan thoroughly with a clean cloth. It's best to do this immediately and to make sure it's absolutely dry before you move on to the next step: put it on the stove top over a low flame for a few minutes. It really needs to be dry.

3   Using a clean cloth (or your fingers), coat the entire pan—inside and out, including the handle—with a thin layer of oil, making sure to really rub it in. The pan should absorb the oil and it should not seem at all greasy. Ideally, you want to use flaxseed oil, but vegetable oil works too. Flaxseed oil is expensive and doesn't have a very long shelf life, so make sure to refrigerate what remains of the bottle and use it within 6 months (it's great in salad dressings and smoothies).

4   Place a baking sheet or just a large piece of foil on the lower rack in your oven; this will prevent any drips from causing a mess later. Place the oiled pan, upside down, on the upper rack and heat the oven to 450°F. Let it bake for 30 minutes. During this time, it may get a little smoky, so make sure to have the vent on or a window open.

5   Remove the pan from the oven and let it cool completely. This should take about 45 minutes.

6   Repeat Steps 3 to 5 three times. Yes, that says three times.

When the fourth round is finished, your pan is seasoned. When it's cooled, wipe it again with a clean cloth. The oil will have chemically reacted to the heat and become polymerized, so the surfaces will be dark black and slightly shiny.

PRE-SEASONED CAST-IRON COOKWARE

Several manufacturers, including Lodge, sell pans that have been pre-seasoned. What that means is that the pan has been heat-treated with oil to create a seasoned layer. When you get it home, you should still wash it gently with warm, soapy water and dry it completely before using for the first time. Like all pan seasoning, it will still need to be re-seasoned when it seems to be wearing off. That will depend on how often you use the pan, how often you cook with oil—frying is a great way to keep your pans seasoned—and how vigorously you clean it. How does one determine that it is time to re-season?

1   Food starts to stick to the surface.

2   The surface seems dull.

It's that simple. Treat a pan that was purchased with seasoning the same way you would a pan that you seasoned yourself after the first year of use.

ENAMELED CAST-IRON COOKWARE

When we talk about cast-iron cookware in this book, we're mostly referring to raw, seasoned iron. The matte black kind. But that isn't the only game in town. Enameled cast-iron pots and pans have been coated with a very durable outer layer of enamel and come in a rainbow of colors. The original enameled cast-iron pans, created at the end of the seventeenth century, were designed to create a smooth cooking surface. Enameled cast iron has lower thermal conductivity than raw cast iron, so it heats more slowly, and doesn't retain heat as long. The enameled surface doesn't ever need to be seasoned but you need to be more conscious of possible chipping, discoloration, and pitting.

Never use enameled cast iron over a campfire.

An enameled pot or pan will cost more than raw cast iron, but you are paying for craftsmanship and, usually, a lifetime warranty. It doesn't rust, but it may chip if you use metal utensils. It also does not add iron to your diet, which for some people is a benefit of using cast iron. Enameled cast iron is an easier material to maintain in the long run and is a good choice for cooking acidic foods, too.

METRIC CONVERSIONS

U.S. Measurement	Approximate Metric Liquid Measurement	Approximate Metric Dry Measurement
1 teaspoon	5 ml	5 g
1 tablespoon or ½ ounce	15 ml	14 g
1 ounce or ⅛ cup	30 ml	29 g
¼ cup or 2 ounces	60 ml	57 g
⅓ cup	80 ml	76 g
½ cup or 4 ounces	120 ml	113 g
⅔ cup	160 ml	151 g
¾ cup or 6 ounces	180 ml	170 g
1 cup or 8 ounces or ½ pint	240 ml	227 g
1½ cups or 12 ounces	350 ml	340 g
2 cups or 1 pint or 16 ounces	475 ml	454 g
3 cups or 1½ pints	700 ml	680 g
4 cups or 2 pints or 1 quart	950 ml	908 g

INDEX

ABOUT CIDER MILL PRESS BOOK PUBLISHERS

❄ ❄ ❄

Good ideas ripen with time. From seed to harvest,
Cider Mill Press brings fine reading, information, and
entertainment together between the covers of its creatively
crafted books. Our Cider Mill bears fruit twice a year,
publishing a new crop of titles each spring and fall.

"Where Good Books Are Ready for Press"

Visit us online at
cidermillpress.com
or write to us at
PO Box 454
12 Spring St.
Kennebunkport, Maine 04046

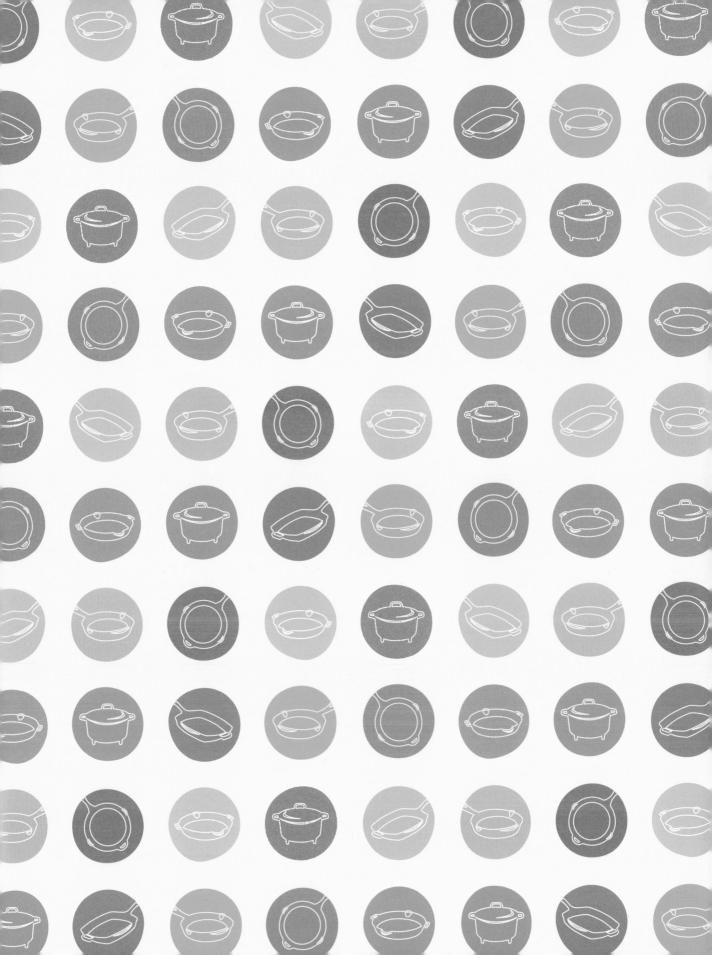